HANDWRITING

Book C

Manuscript Writing
Now I can write letters, words, and sentences.

Thomas M. Wasylyk

Copyright © 2013, All Rights Reserved

Book C, Item #132, ISBN 978-1-931181-59-4

IT IS ILLEGAL TO PHOTOCOPY THIS BOOK

This book is not to be reproduced in any manner whatsoever, in part or whole, without the written permission of the publisher. For additional information contact Universal Publishing.

1-800-940-2270 • www.upub.net

Manuscript Alphabet

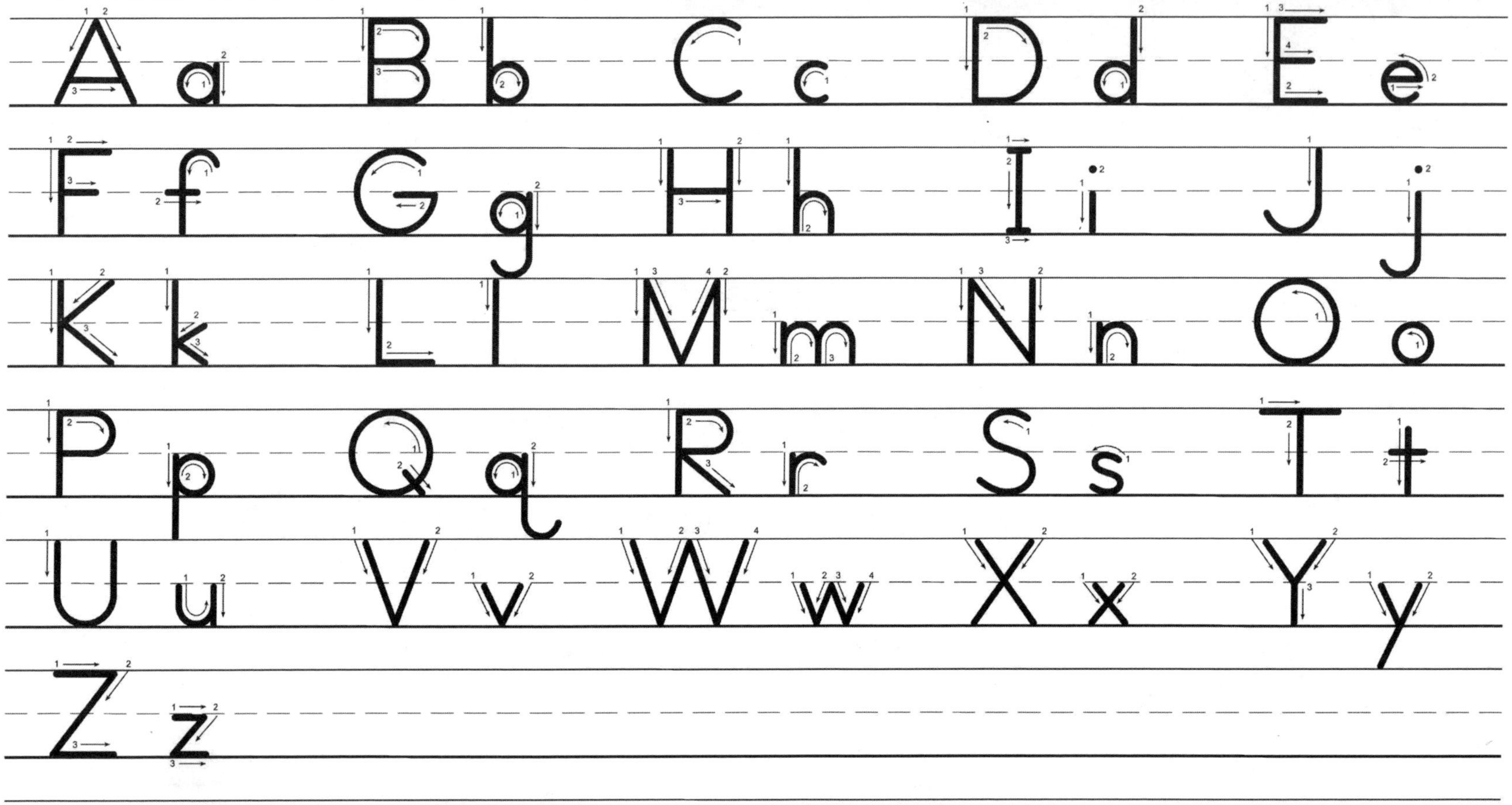

Aa Bb Cc Dd Ee
Ff Gg Hh Ii Jj
Kk Ll Mm Nn Oo
Pp Qq Rr Ss Tt
Uu Vv Ww Xx Yy
Zz

Punctuation and Numbers

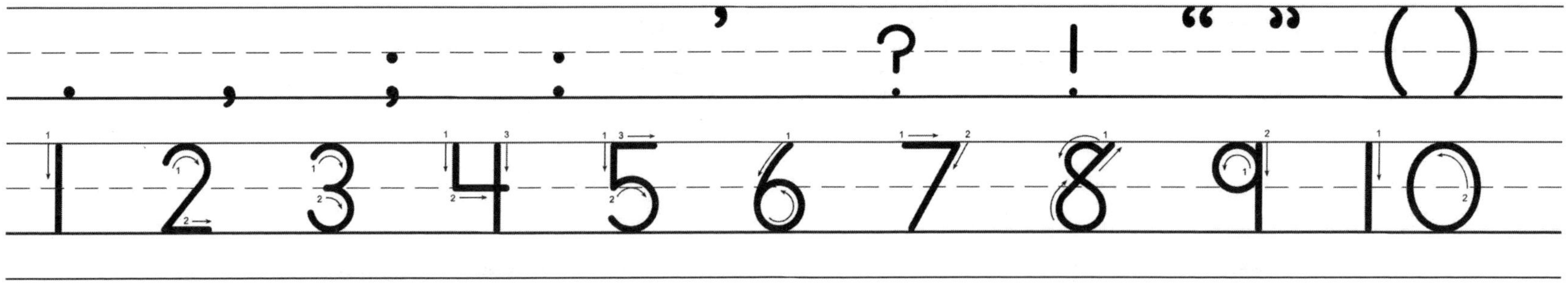

. , ; : ? ! " " ( )

1 2 3 4 5 6 7 8 9 10

GOOD POSTURE

1. Both feet on the floor
2. Elbows off the edge of desk
3. Sit back in chair
4. Shoulders slightly forward
5. Proper desk height

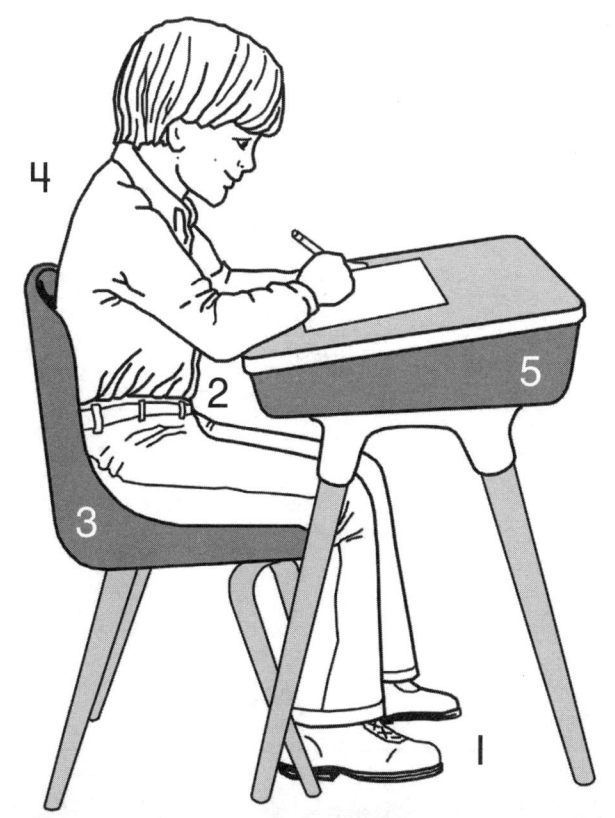

GOOD HANDWRITING

PAPER POSITION

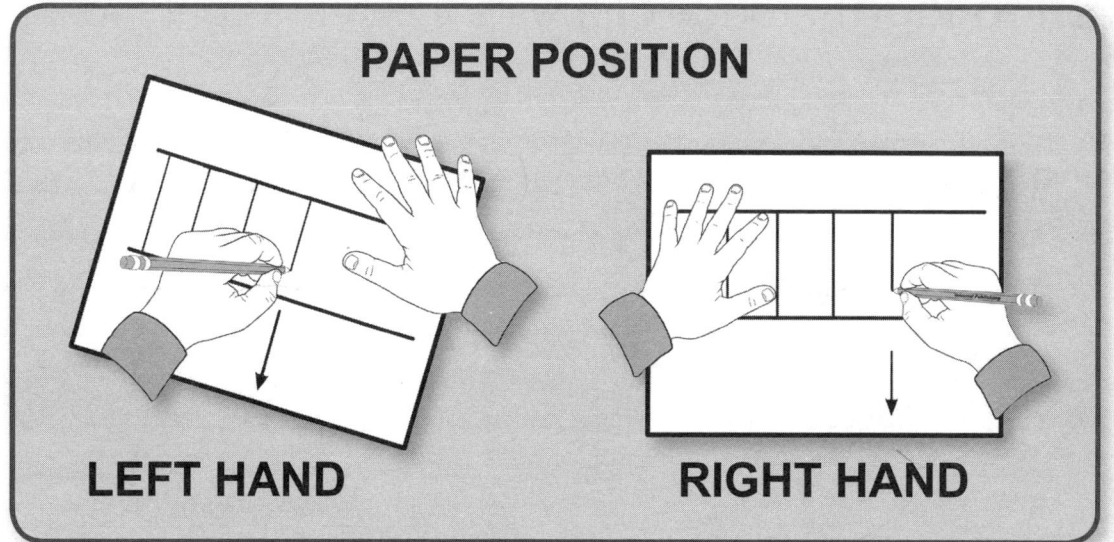

LEFT HAND   **RIGHT HAND**

Pencil Position

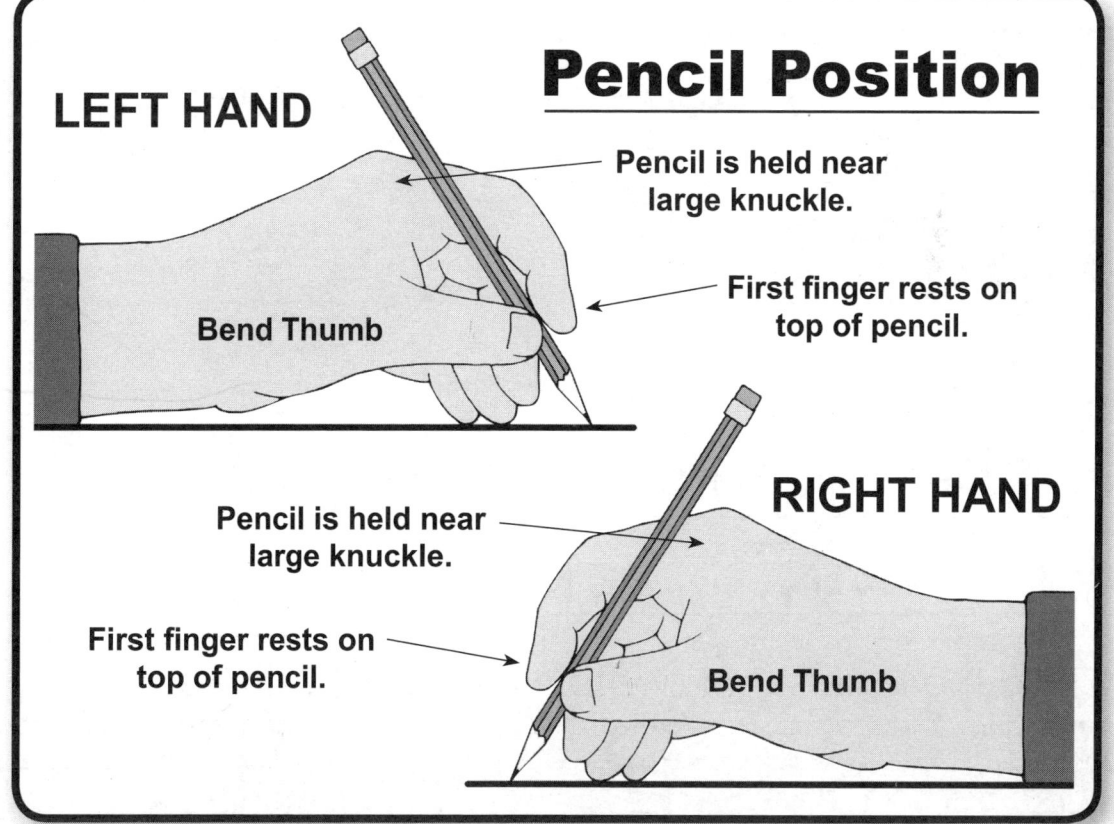

LEFT HAND
- Pencil is held near large knuckle.
- First finger rests on top of pencil.
- Bend Thumb

RIGHT HAND
- Pencil is held near large knuckle.
- First finger rests on top of pencil.
- Bend Thumb

Left to Right Trace and write the left-to-right strokes.

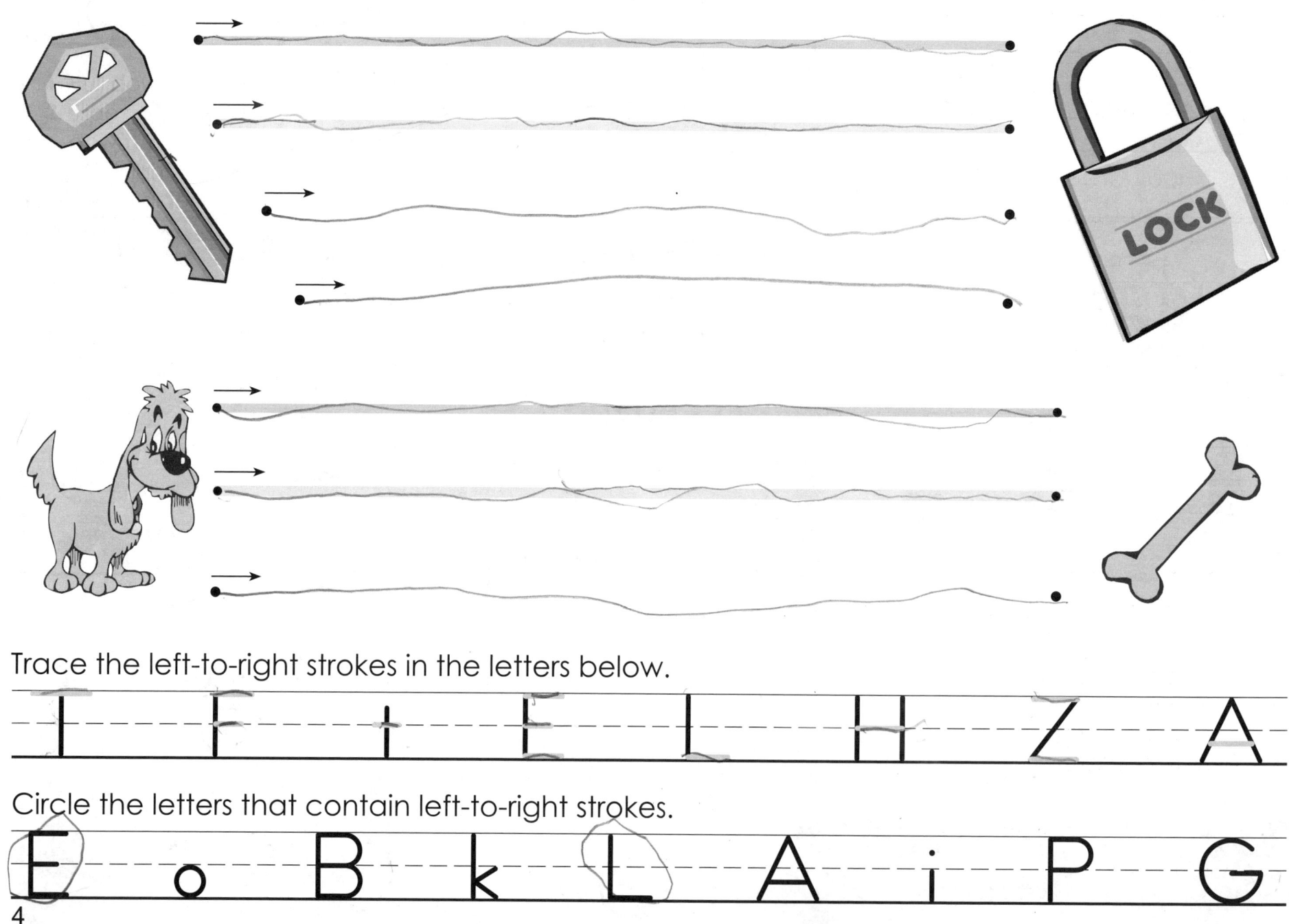

Trace the left-to-right strokes in the letters below.

I E t E L H Z A

Circle the letters that contain left-to-right strokes.

E o B k L A i P G

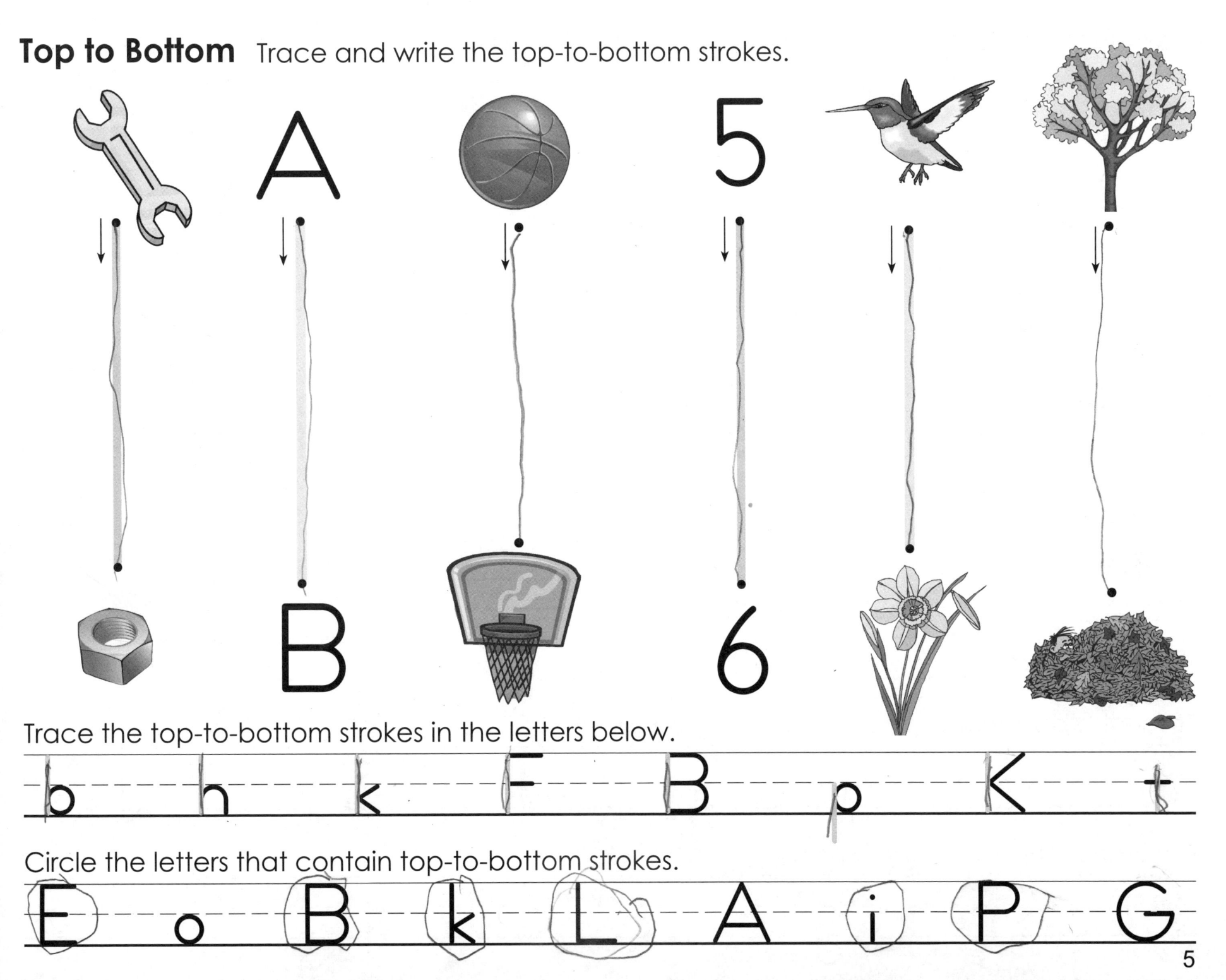

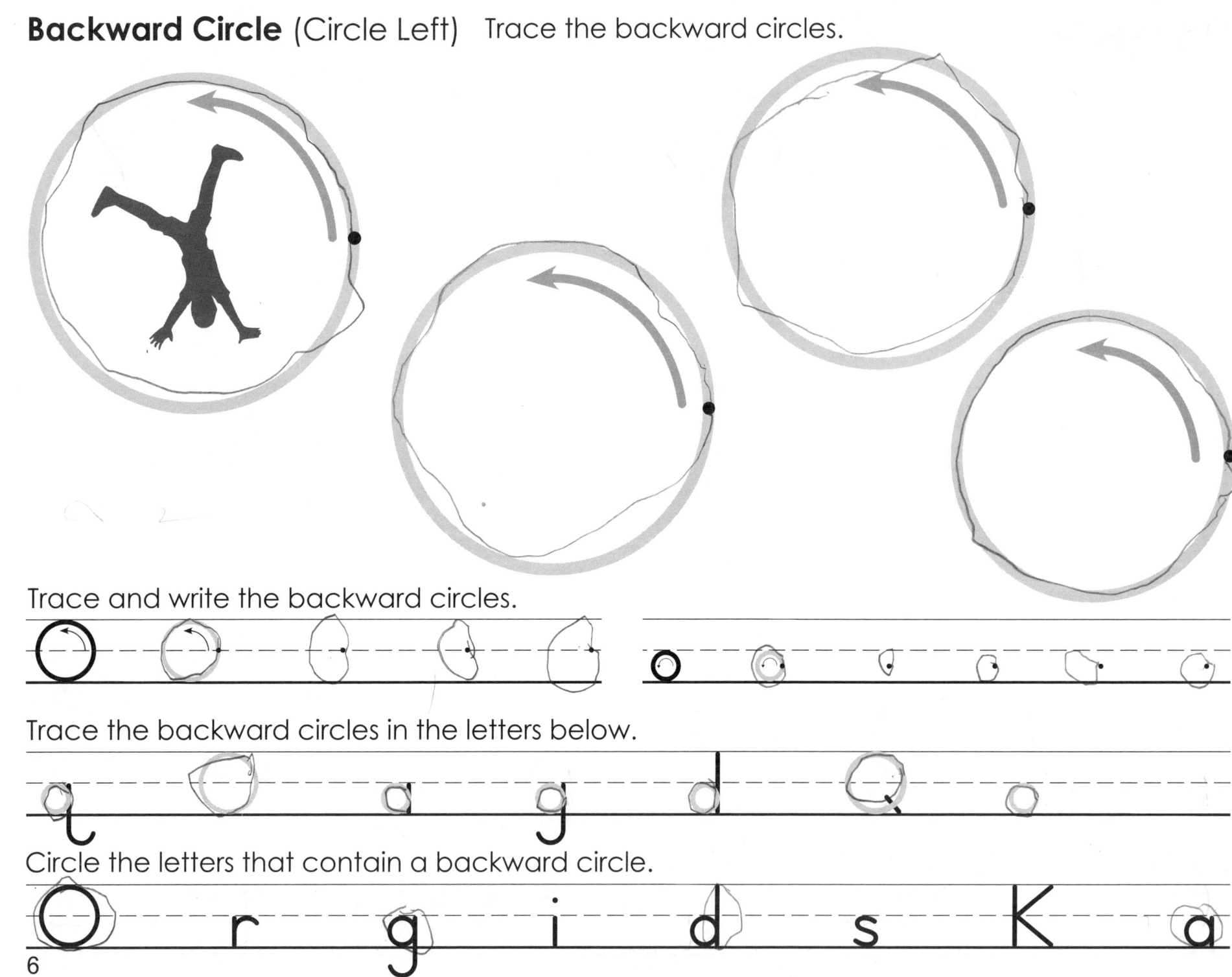

Forward Circle (Circle Right)   Trace the forward circles.

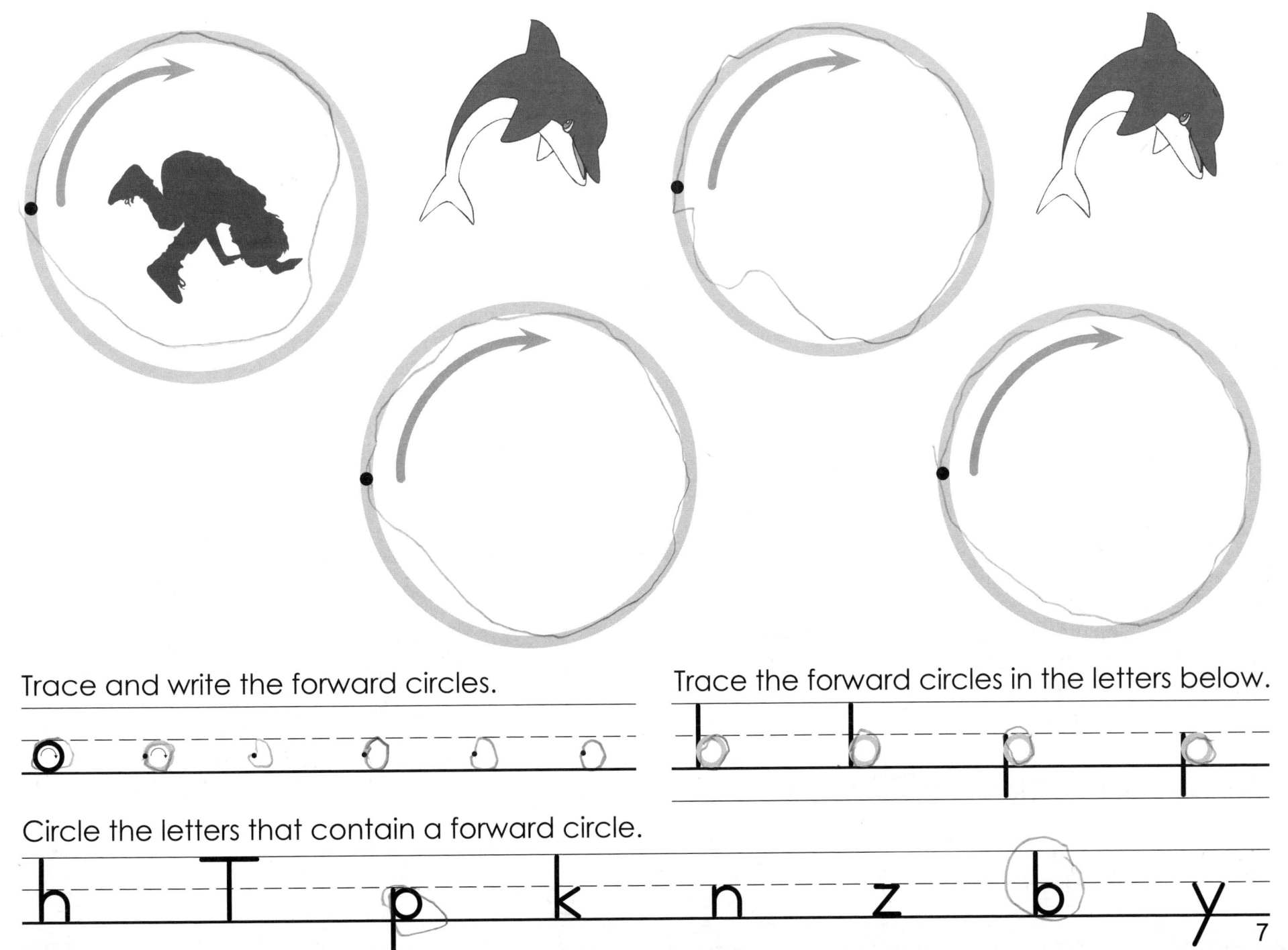

Trace and write the forward circles.

Trace the forward circles in the letters below.

Circle the letters that contain a forward circle.

h T p k n z b y

Slant Right
Trace and write the slant-right strokes.

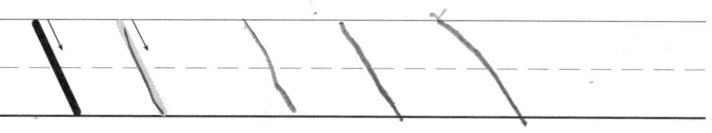
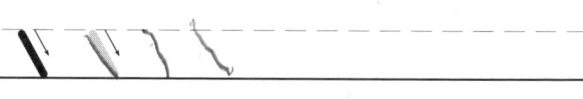

Trace the slant-right strokes in the letters below.

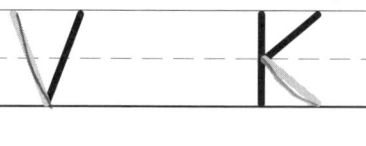  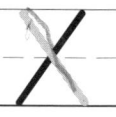  

Slant Left
Trace and write the slant-left strokes.

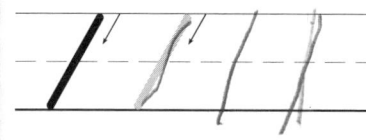

Trace the slant-left strokes in the letters below.

 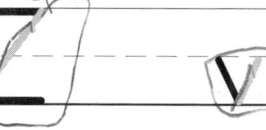 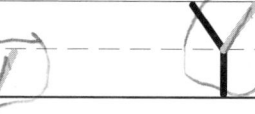 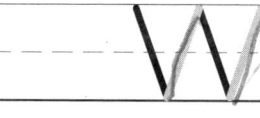 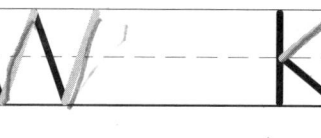 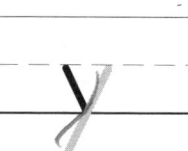 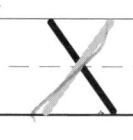

Circle the letters that contain a slant stroke.

 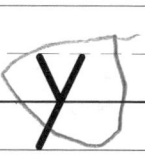   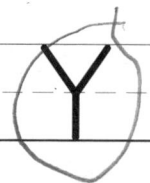 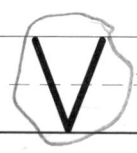  

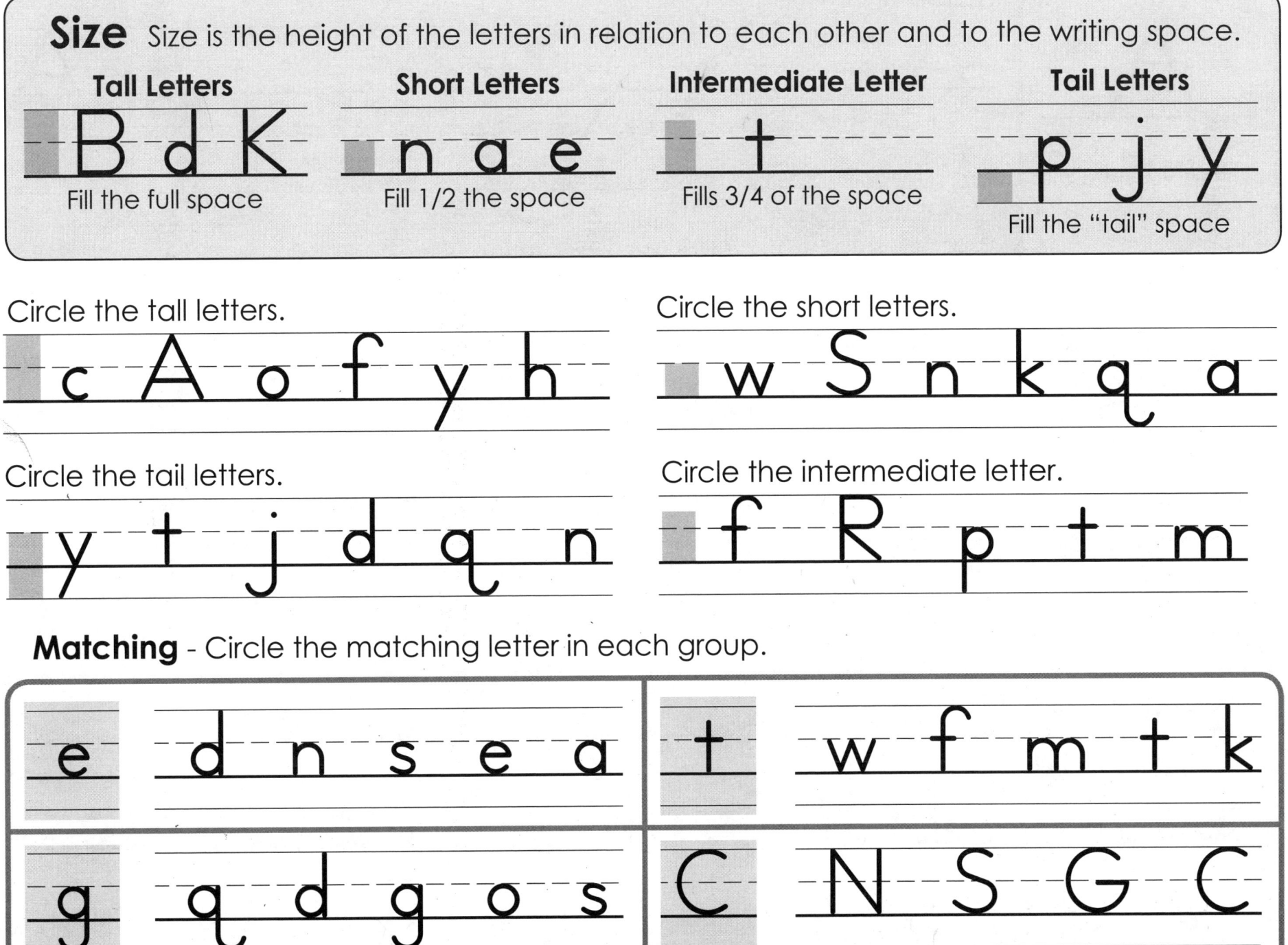

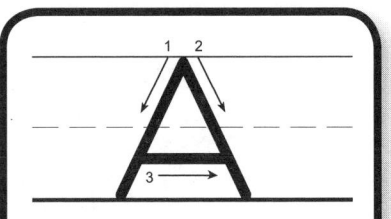

1. Slant left
2. Slant right
3. Slide right

Trace and write the letter.

Trace and write the words.

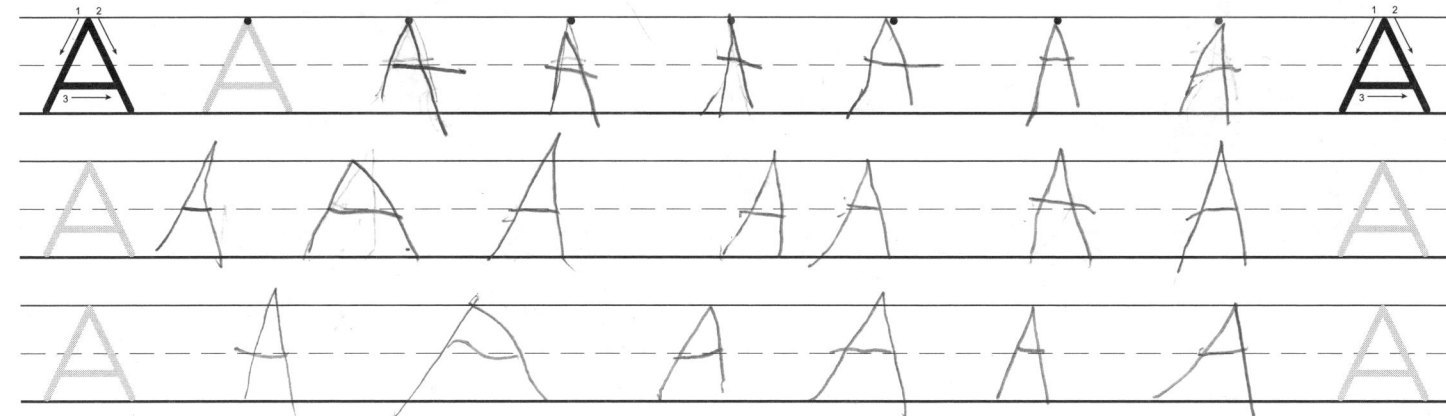

Spacing between Letters
The words below show correct letter spacing. Write the words. Check your letter spacing.

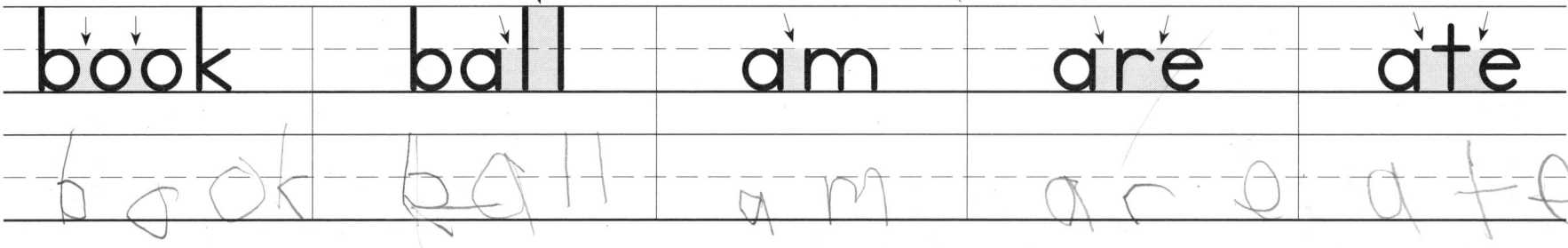

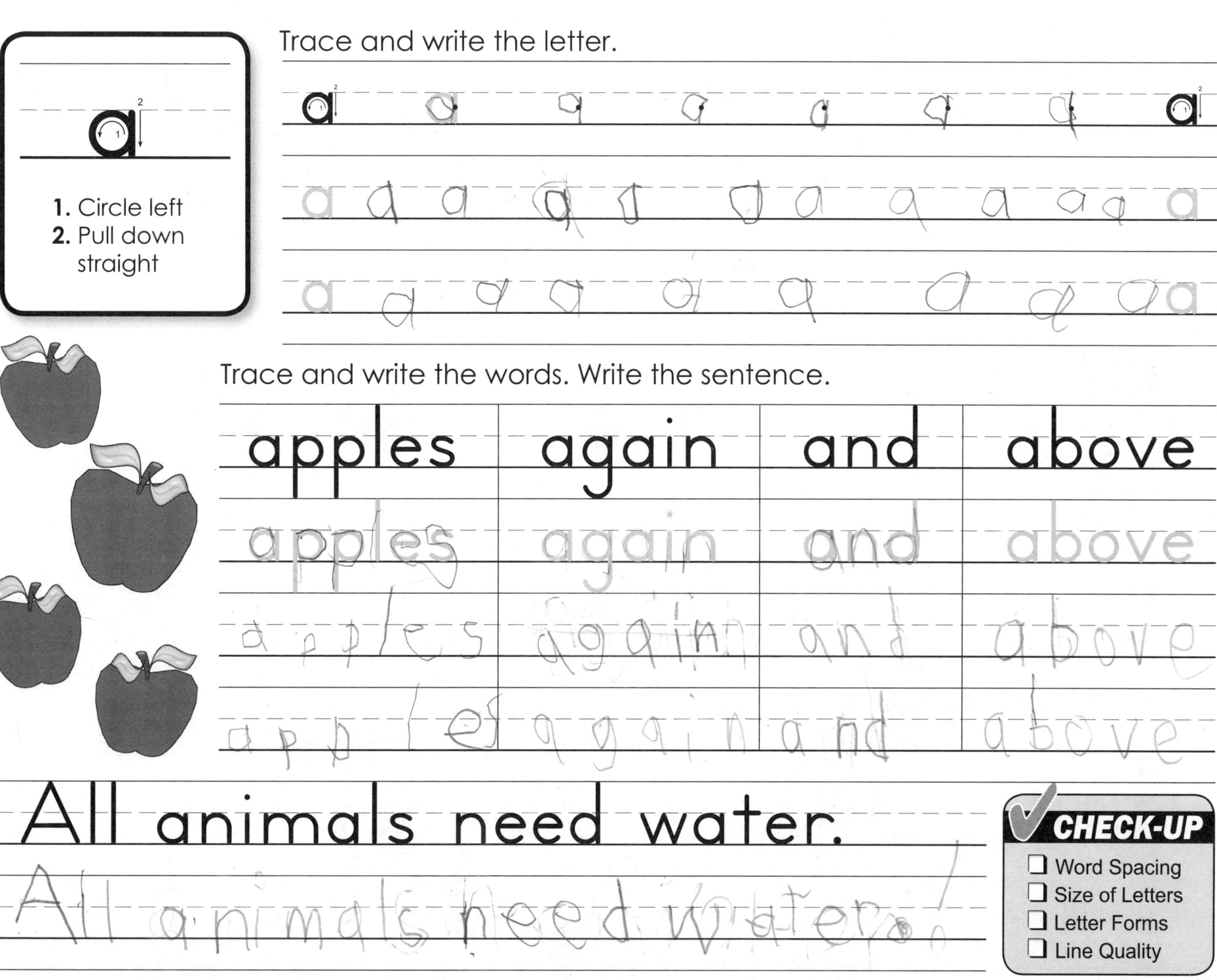

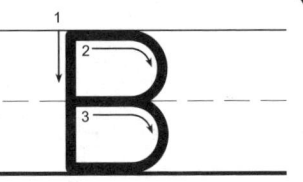

1. Pull down straight
2. Slide right, curve down, slide left
3. Slide right, curve down, slide left

Trace and write the letter.

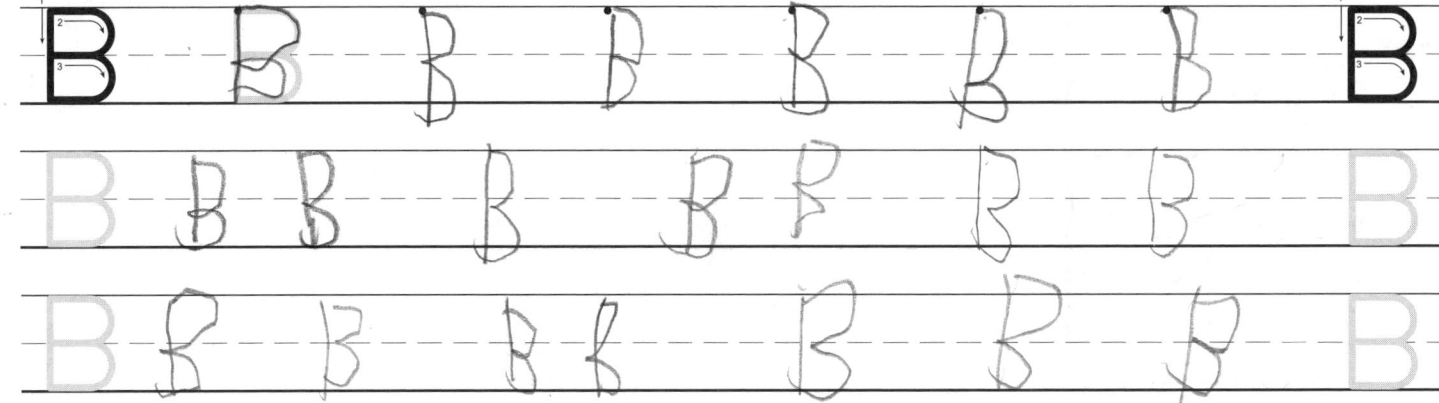

Trace and write the words.

Ben	Barb	Billy	Brooke
Ben	Barb	Billy	Brooke
Ben			

Alignment

Alignment is the evenness of letters along the baseline and along their tops. All letters of the same size should be even in height.

CORRECT

ball

INCORRECT

ball

Write the sentence. Check your alignment.

Brian, bring your bat.

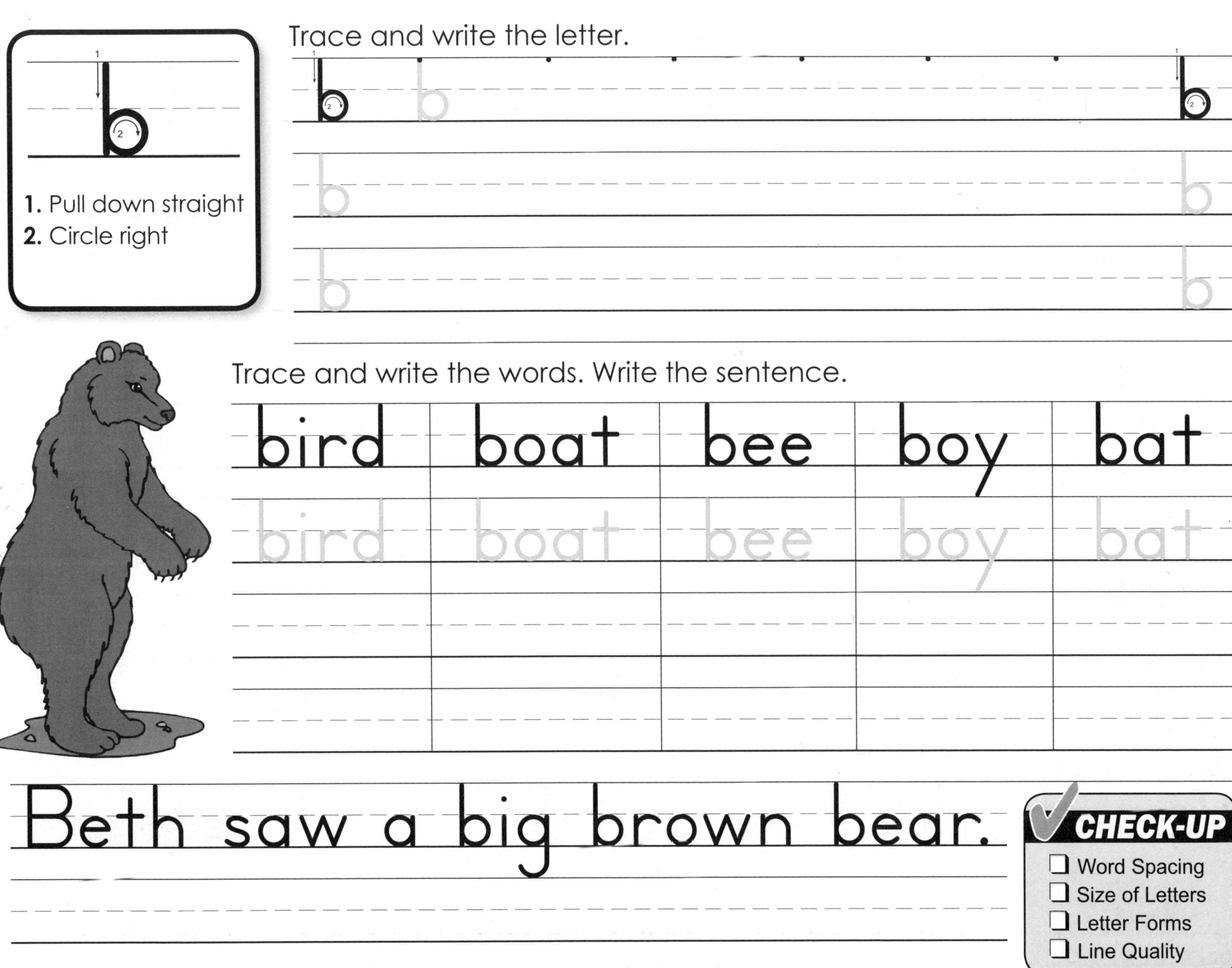

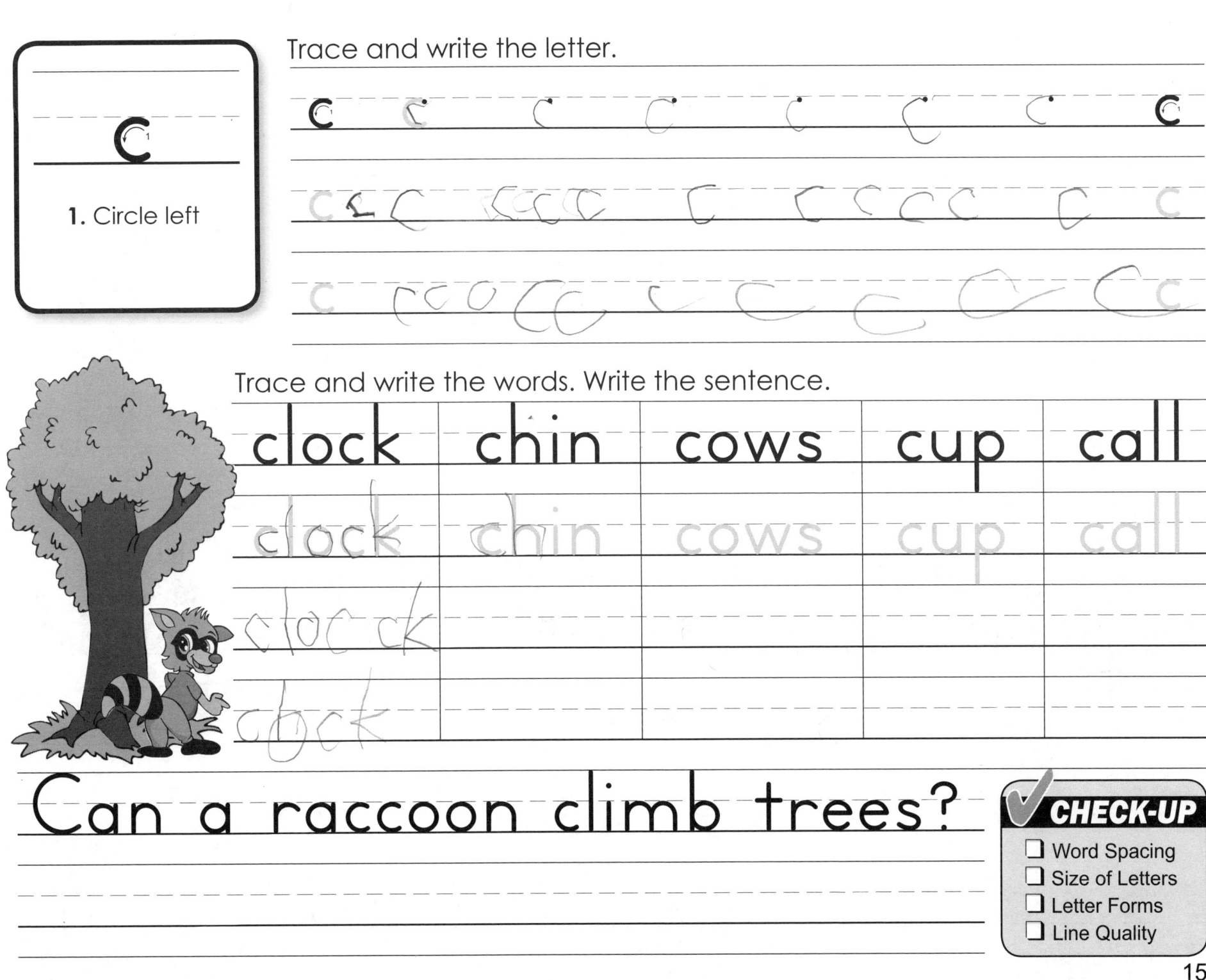

Statue of Liberty

Write the sentence.

France gave the Statue of

Liberty to the U. S. in 1886.

Write the sentences.

**The Statue of Liberty is on Liberty Island.
She is 152 feet tall from feet to torch.**

The Bald Eagle

Write the sentences.

The bald eagle is the United States national bird. It is a symbol of freedom and strength.

 ☐ Word Spacing ☐ Size of Letters ☐ Letter Forms ☐ Line Quality ☐ Letter Spacing

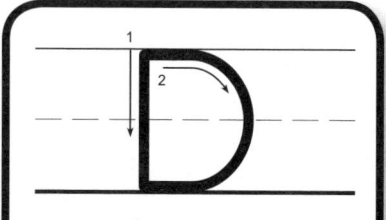

1. Pull down straight
2. Slide right, curve down, slide left

Trace and write the letter.

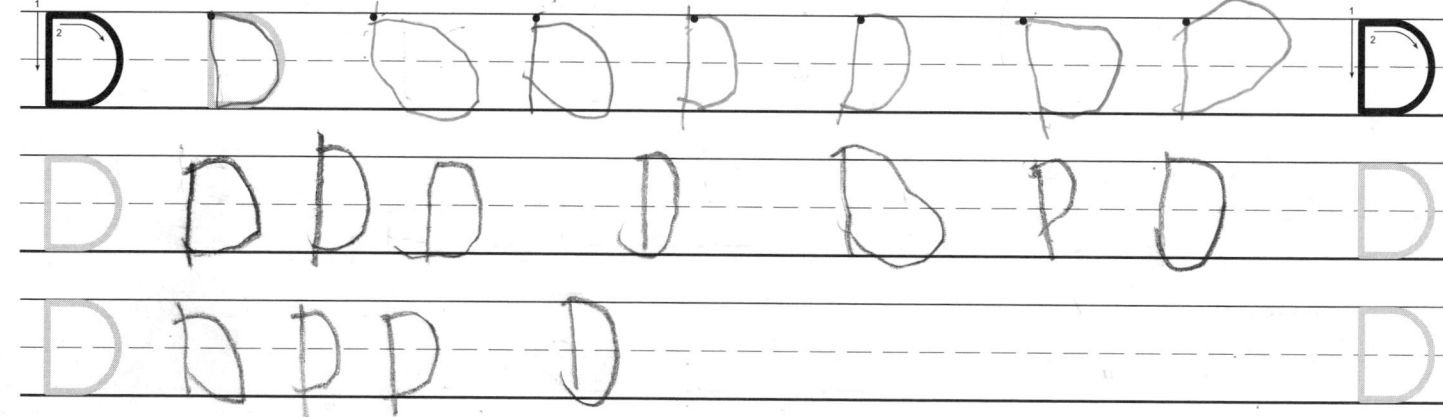

Trace and write the words.

Delaware	December	Dad	Drew
Delaware	December	Dad	Drew
Del			

Word Spacing — Allow enough space between words for one lowercase **o**. Write the sentence. Check your word spacing.

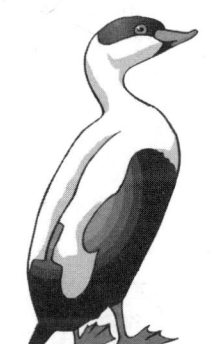

Ducks swim on our pond.

18

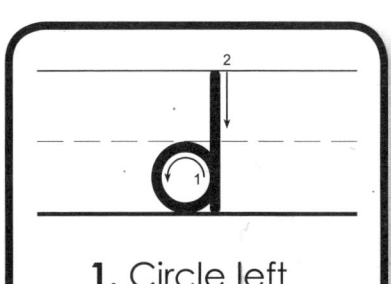

1. Circle left
2. Pull down straight

Trace and write the letter.

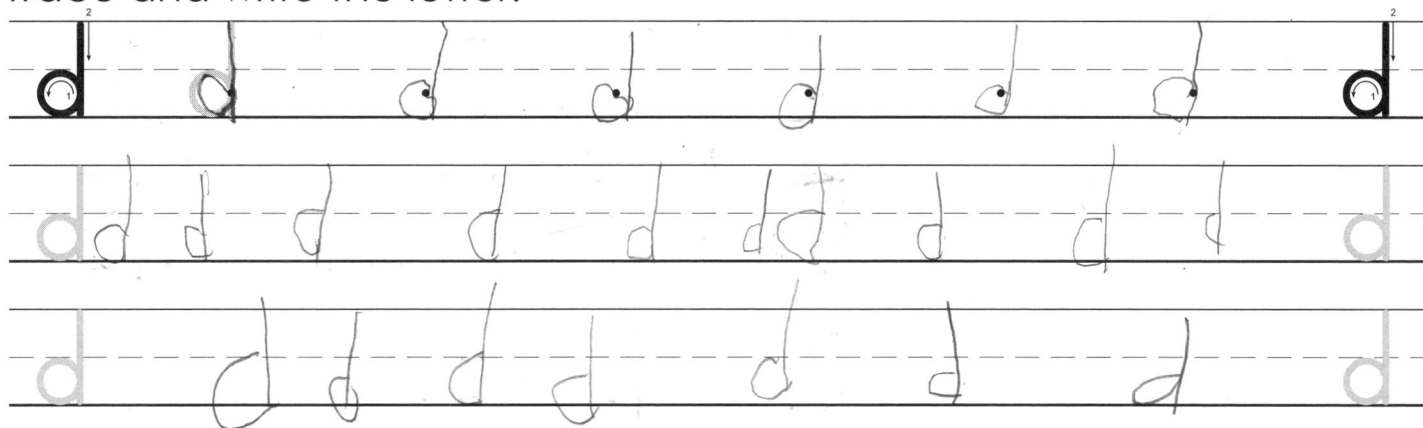

Trace and write the words. Write the sentence.

duck	dime	day	dear	dinner
duck	dime	day	dear	dinner
duck	dime	day		
duck	dime			

Did Daddy drop the dishes?

CHECK-UP
- ☐ Word Spacing
- ☐ Size of Letters
- ☐ Letter Forms
- ☐ Line Quality

19

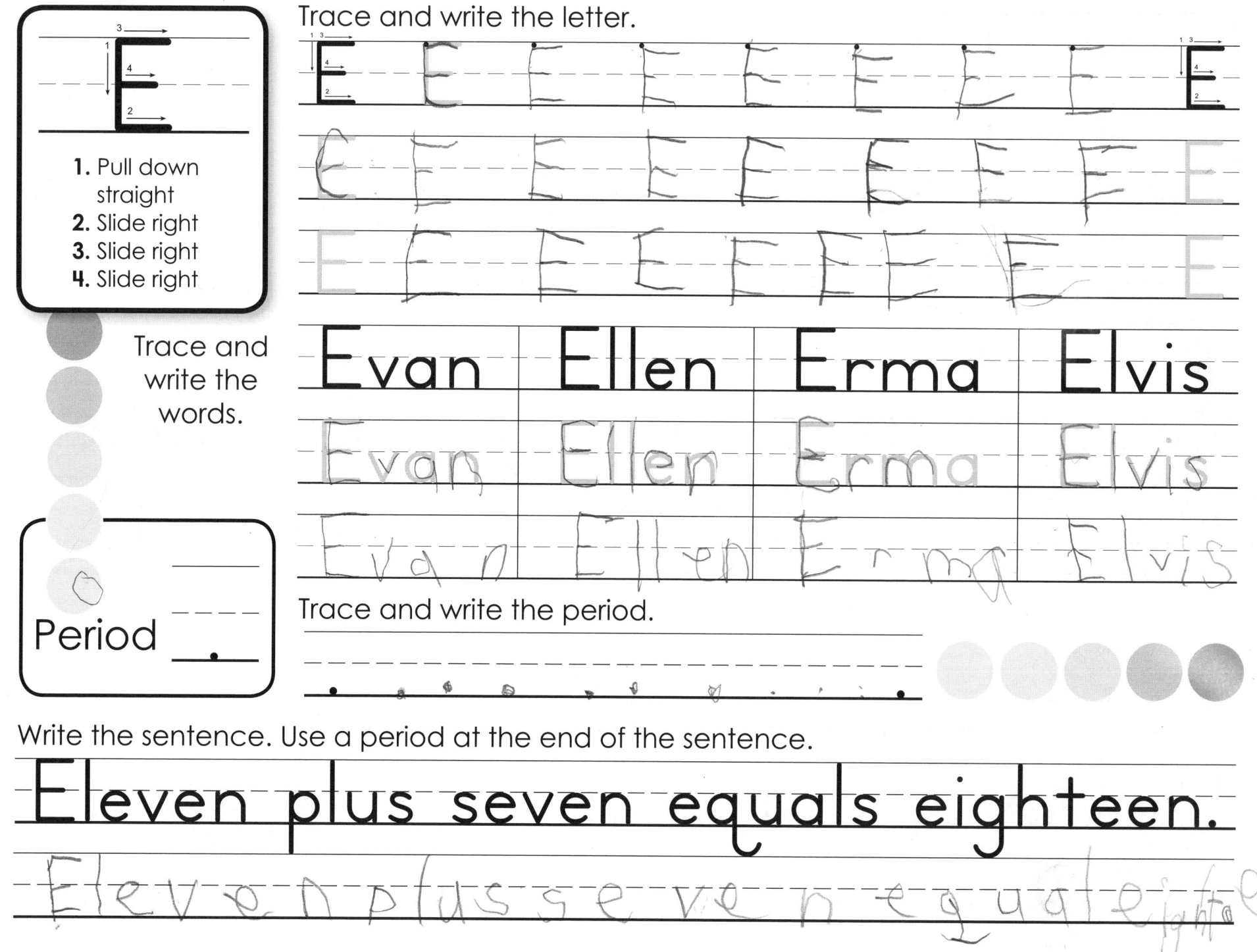

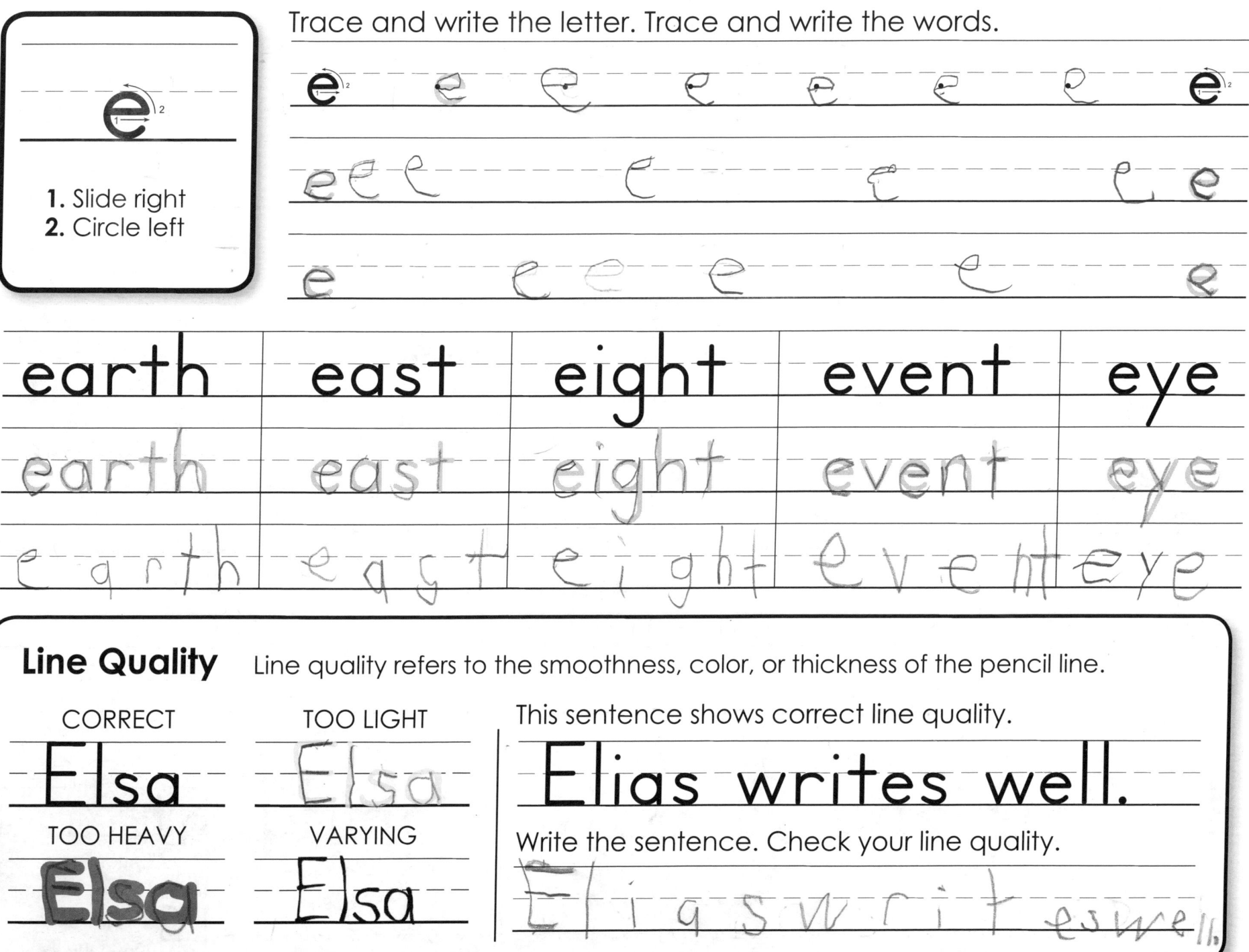

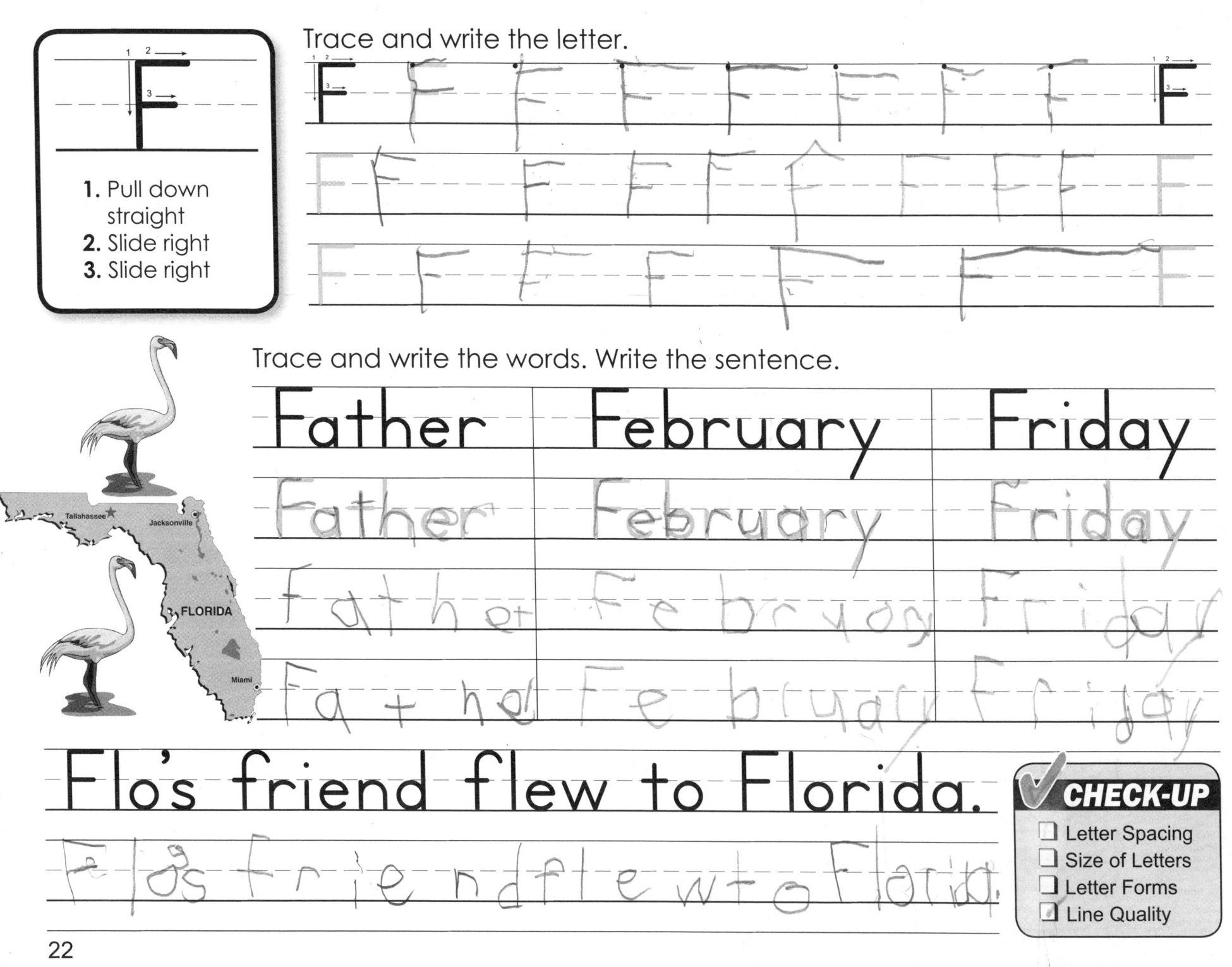

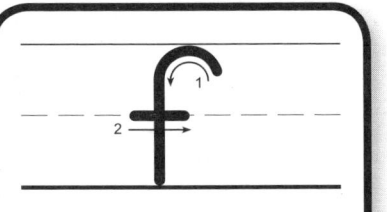

1. Curve left, pull down straight
2. Slide right

Trace and write the letter.

Trace and write the words. Write the sentence.

Jeff found four feathers.

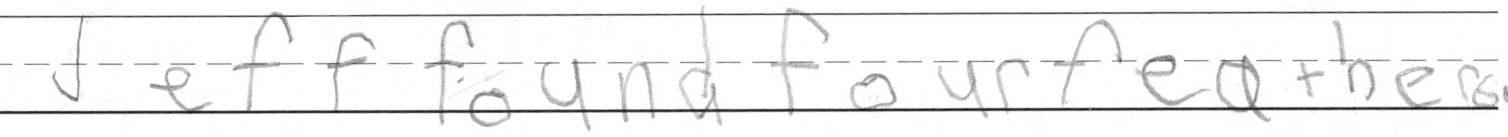

✓ **CHECK-UP**
☐ Word Spacing
☐ Size of Letters
☐ Letter Forms
☐ Line Quality

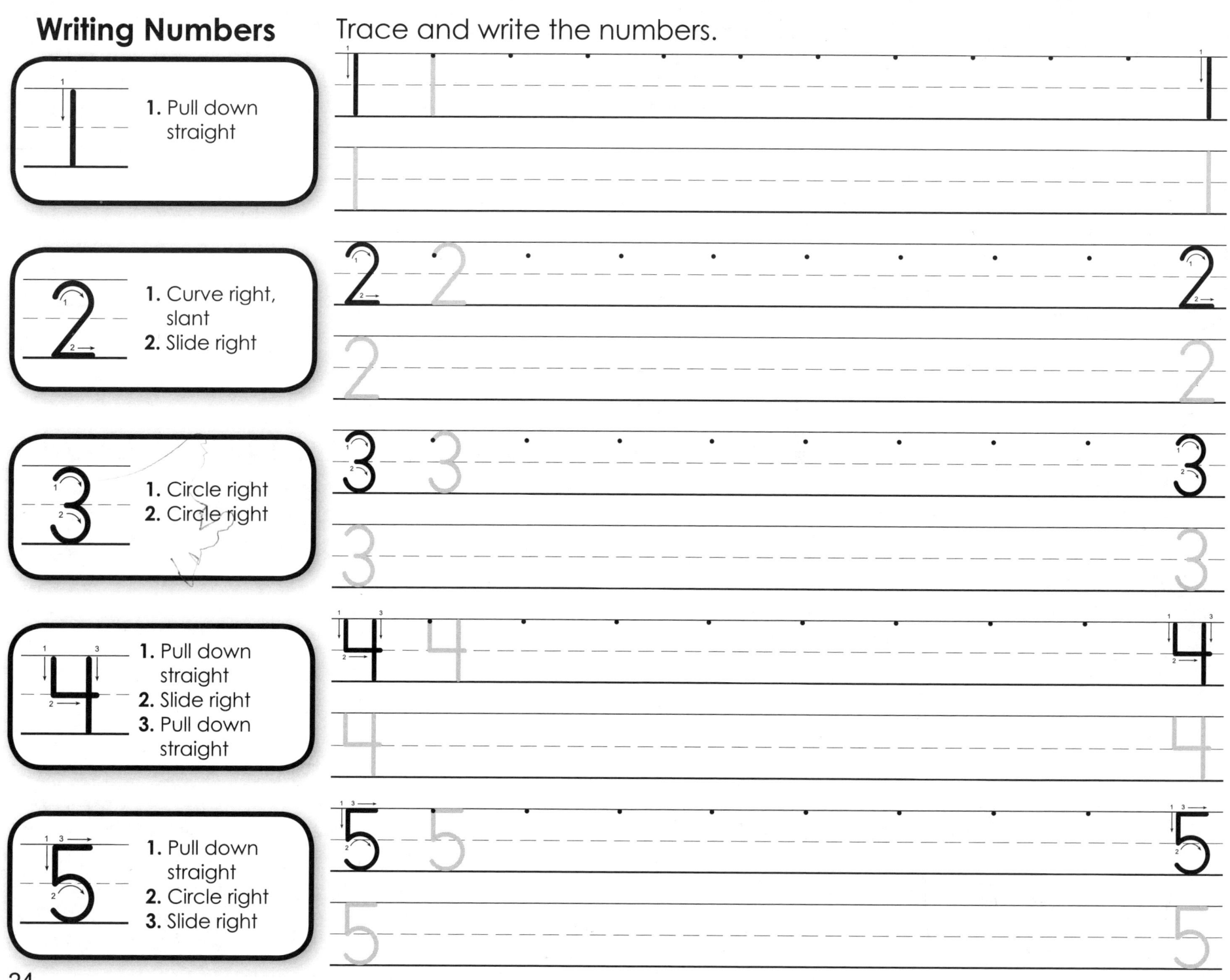

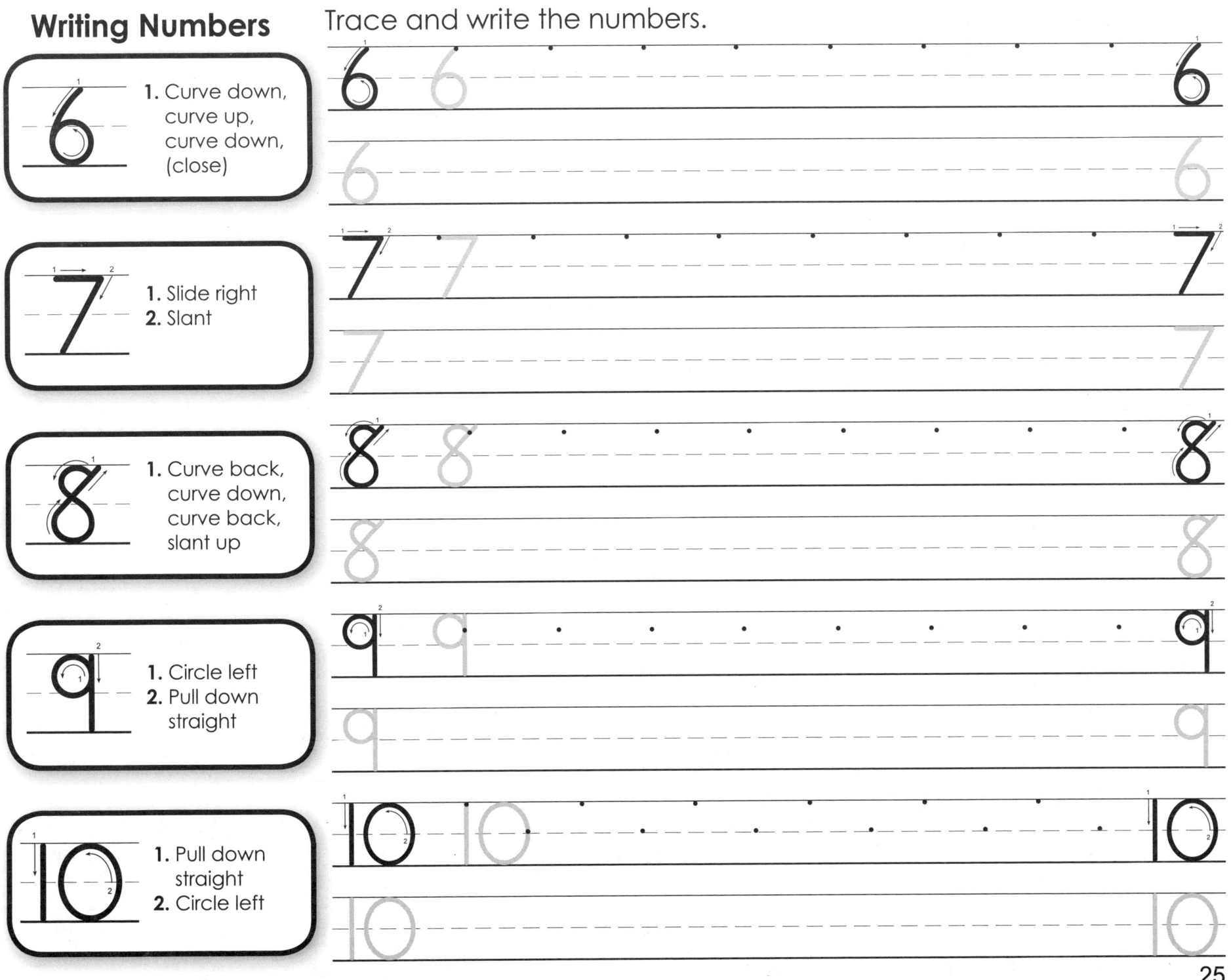

G

1. Circle left
2. Slide left

Trace and write the letter.

G G G

Trace and write the words. Write the sentence.

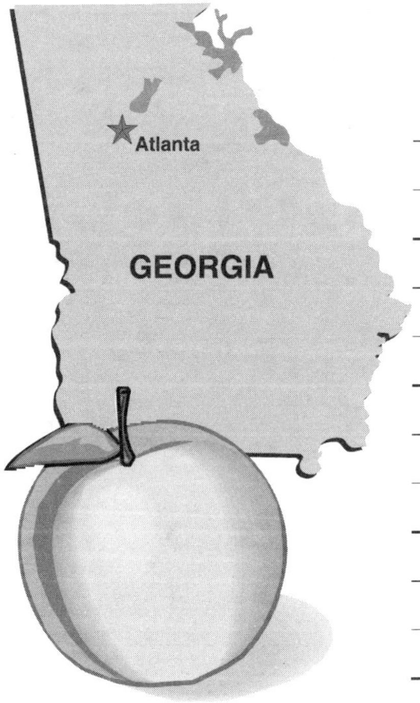

Georgia Greg Ginger

Georgia Greg Ginger

Gary grew up in Germany.

CHECK-UP

- ❑ Letter Spacing
- ❑ Size of Letters
- ❑ Letter Forms
- ❑ Line Quality

Trace and write the letter.

g

1. Circle left
2. Pull down straight, curve left

Trace and write the words. Write the sentence.

| great | goose | girls | goat |

The grasshopper is green.

✓ **CHECK-UP**
☐ Word Spacing
☐ Size of Letters
☐ Letter Forms
☐ Line Quality

Trace and write the letter.

1. Pull down straight
2. Pull down straight
3. Slide right

Trace and write the words. Write the sentence.

Hawaii	Henry	Hillary
Hawaii	Henry	Hillary

His horse is named Harley.

CHECK-UP
☐ Letter Spacing
☐ Size of Letters
☐ Letter Forms
☐ Line Quality

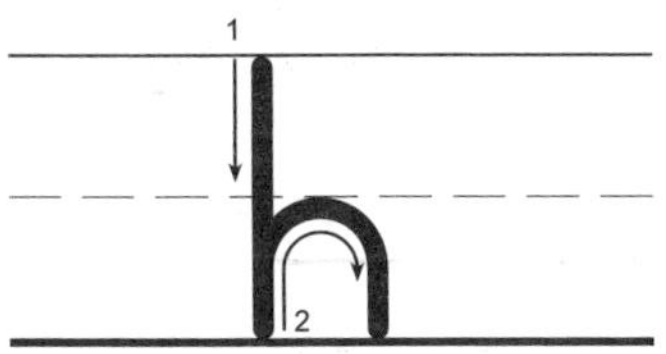

1. Pull down straight
2. Push up, curve right, pull down

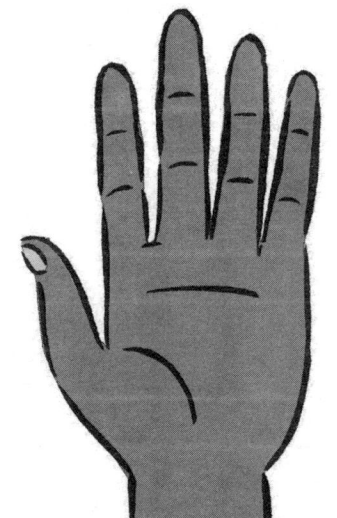

Trace and write the letter.

h h h h

h h

h h

Trace and write the words. Write the sentence.

hand	hot	happy	help
hand	hot	happy	help

Hali has three new shirts.

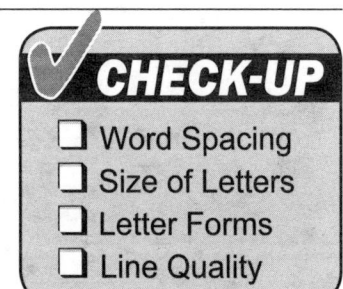

CHECK-UP

- ❑ Word Spacing
- ❑ Size of Letters
- ❑ Letter Forms
- ❑ Line Quality

Writing Numbers

Counting by Fives Fill in the missing numbers.

5 _____ 15 20 _____ 30 _____ 40

45 _____ 55 _____ 65 70 _____

Write the number for each number word below.

twelve _____

sixteen _____

seven _____

fourteen _____

nine _____

twenty _____

| four | eleven | two |
| five | sixteen | eight |

Write the correct word for each number below.

4 _____   8 _____

2 _____   5 _____

11 _____   16 _____

Today's Weather

Draw a picture of what your weather is like today.

Write what you would like to do on a day like today.

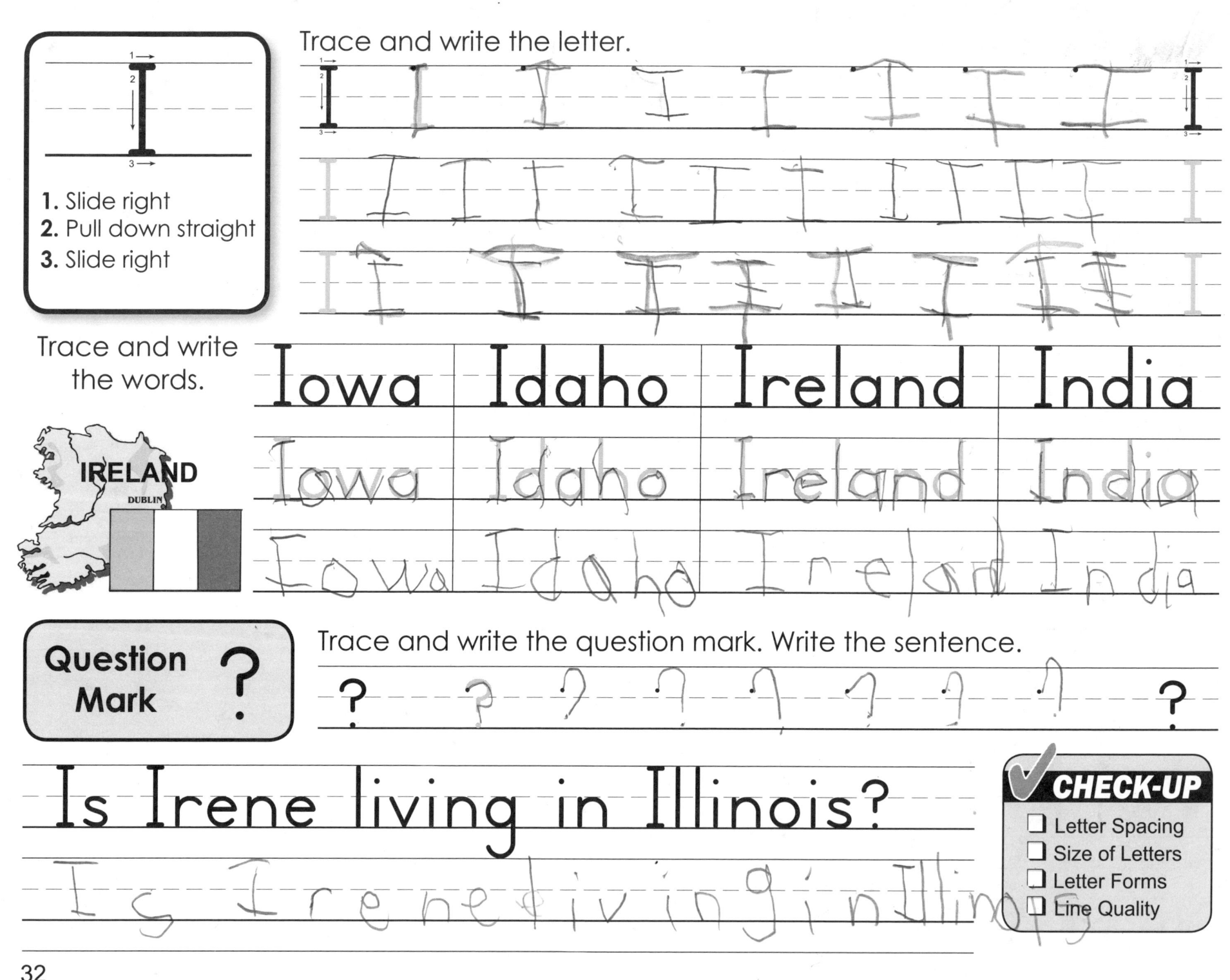

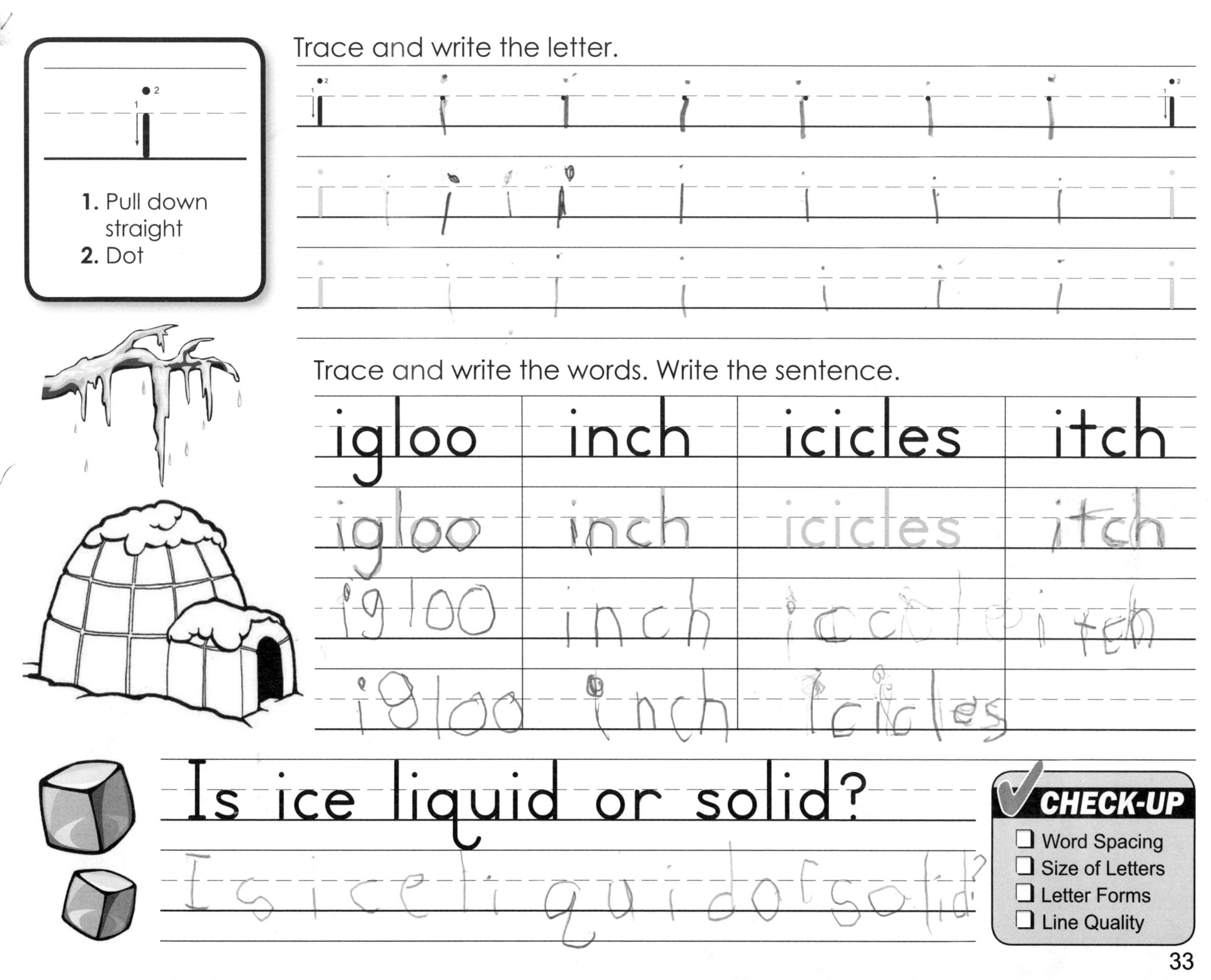

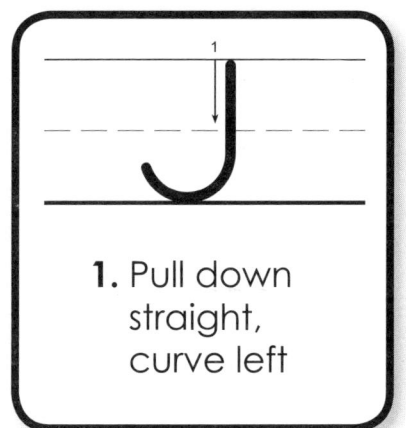

1. Pull down straight, curve left

Trace and write the letter.

J J J

J J

J J

Trace and write the words. Write the sentence.

James	Jackie	January
James	Jackie	January

Jill camps in June or July.

✓ CHECK-UP
☐ Letter Spacing
☐ Size of Letters
☐ Letter Forms
☐ Line Quality

34

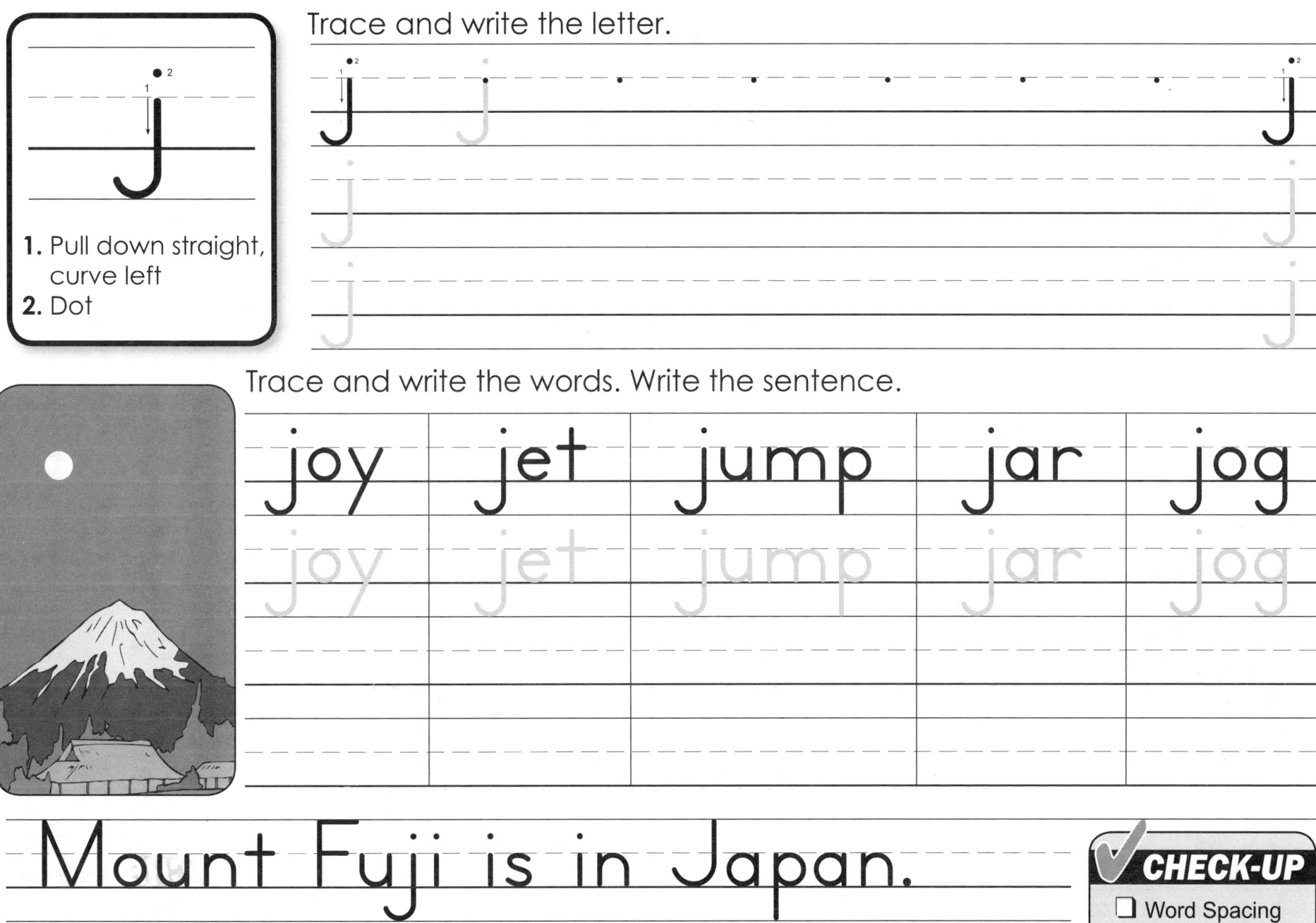

Trace and write the letter.

1. Pull down straight, curve left
2. Dot

Trace and write the words. Write the sentence.

joy   jet   jump   jar   jog

Mount Fuji is in Japan.

CHECK-UP
☐ Word Spacing
☐ Size of Letters
☐ Letter Forms
☐ Line Quality

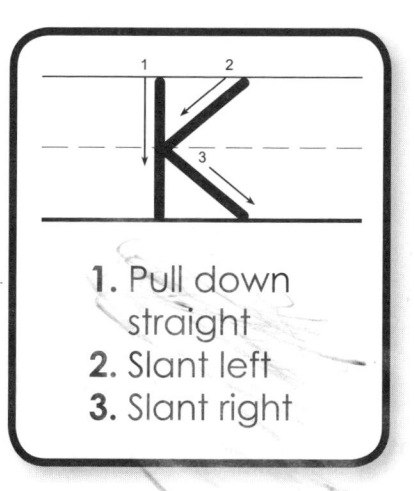

1. Pull down straight
2. Slant left
3. Slant right

Trace and write the letter.

Trace and write the words. Write the sentence.

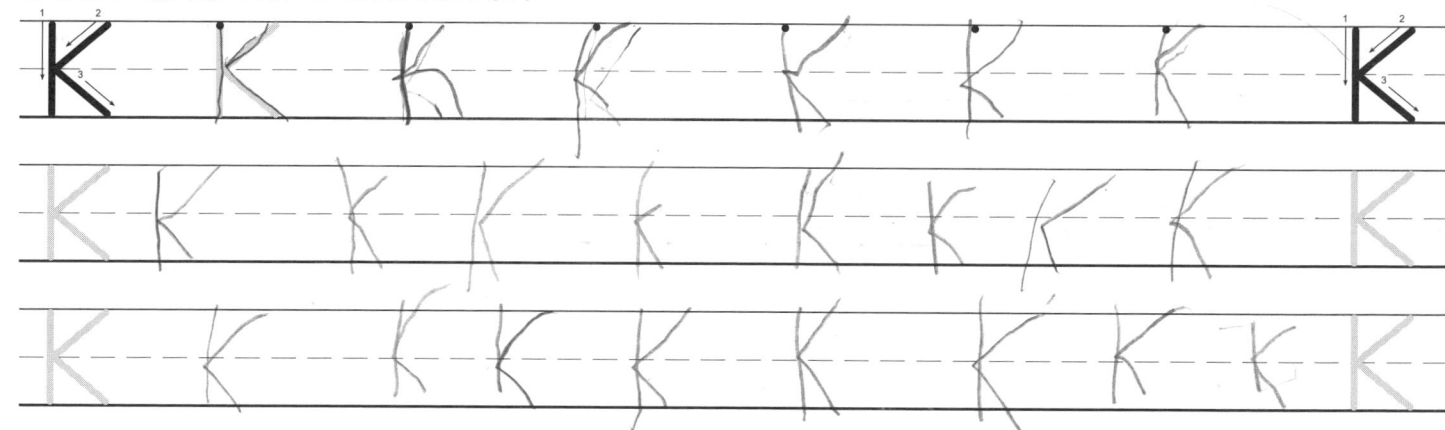

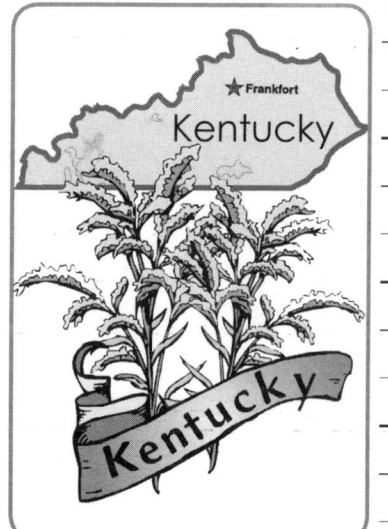

| Kentucky | Kyra | Kirk | Kate |

Kyle went to Kansas City.

✓ CHECK-UP
☐ Letter Spacing
☐ Size of Letters
☐ Letter Forms
☐ Line Quality

36

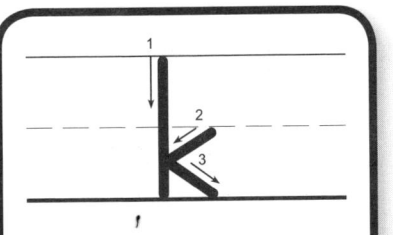

1. Pull down straight
2. Slant left
3. Slant right

Trace and write the letter.

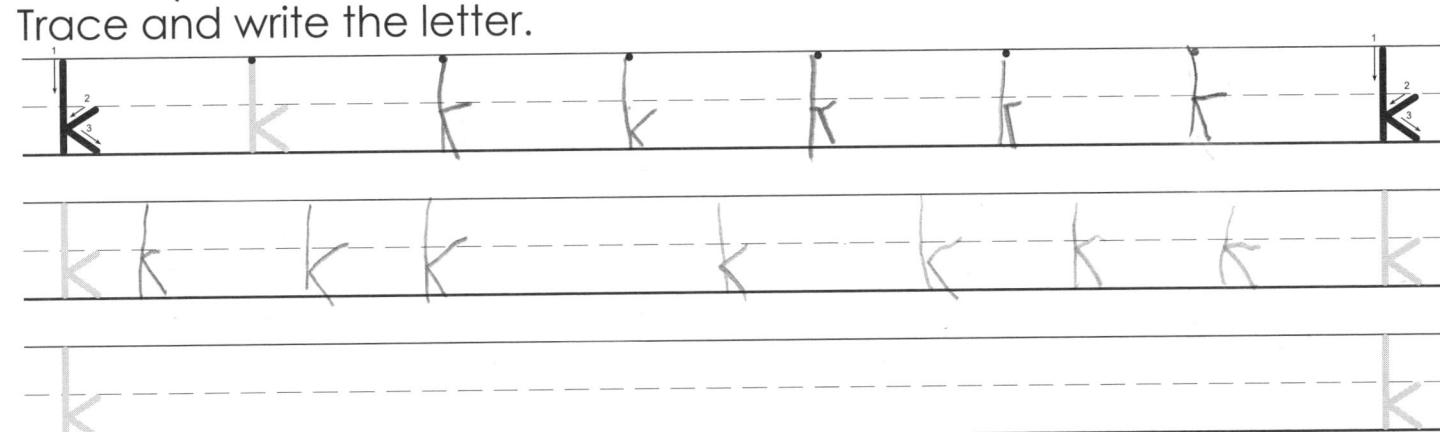

Trace and write the words. Write the sentence.

kick	knee	keep	kittens
kick	knee	keep	kittens
kick			
kick			

Kay kicked the ball to Jack.

✓ CHECK-UP
☐ Word Spacing
☐ Size of Letters
☐ Letter Forms
☐ Line Quality

Plant Parts

Use the words in the box to label the parts of the plant.

leaves

flower

stem

roots

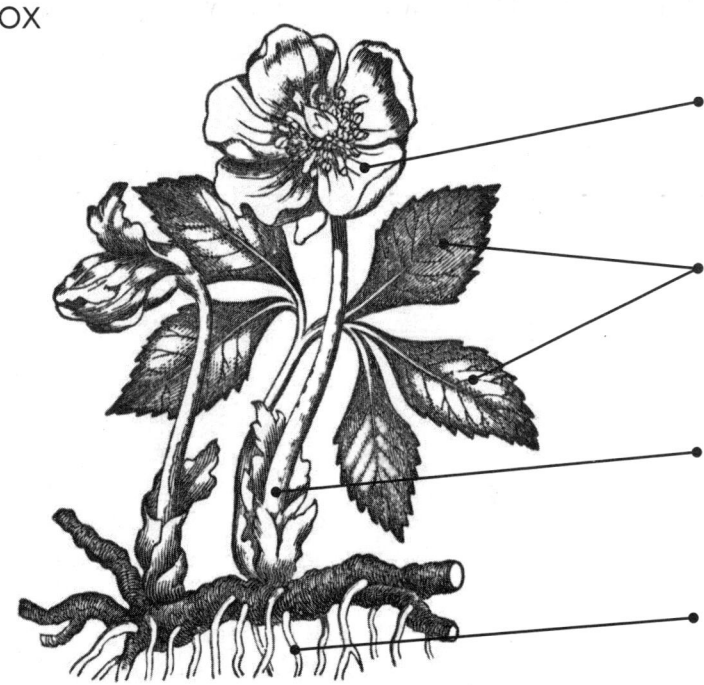

_____
_____
_____
_____

Write the sentence.

A plant's roots hold it to the ground and give the plant water.

Where Do They Live?

Where does each animal live? What helps them survive? Write your answers below.

Polar Bear

Camel

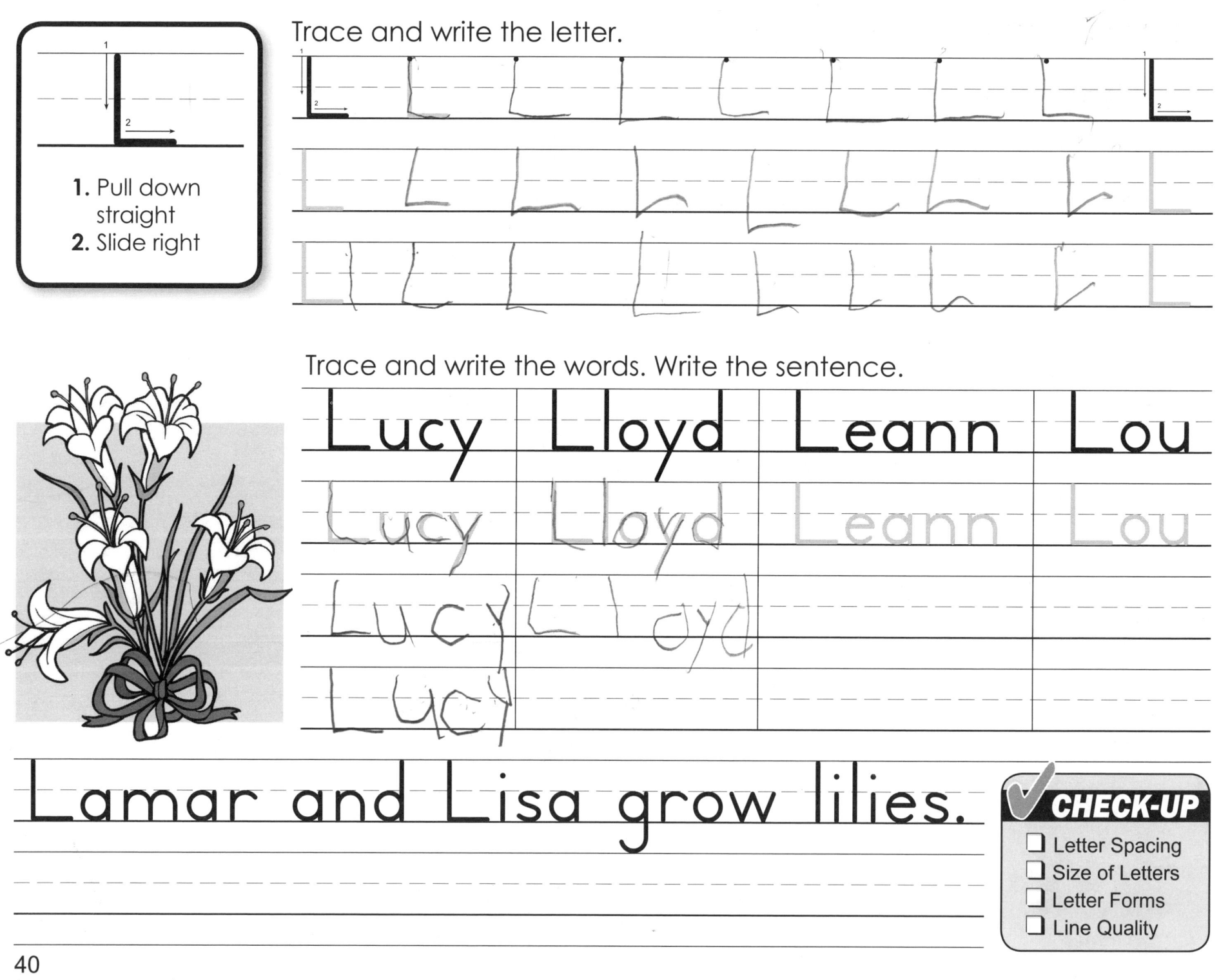

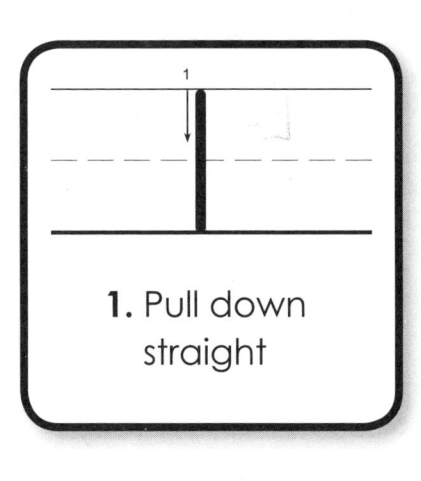

1. Pull down straight

Trace and write the letter.

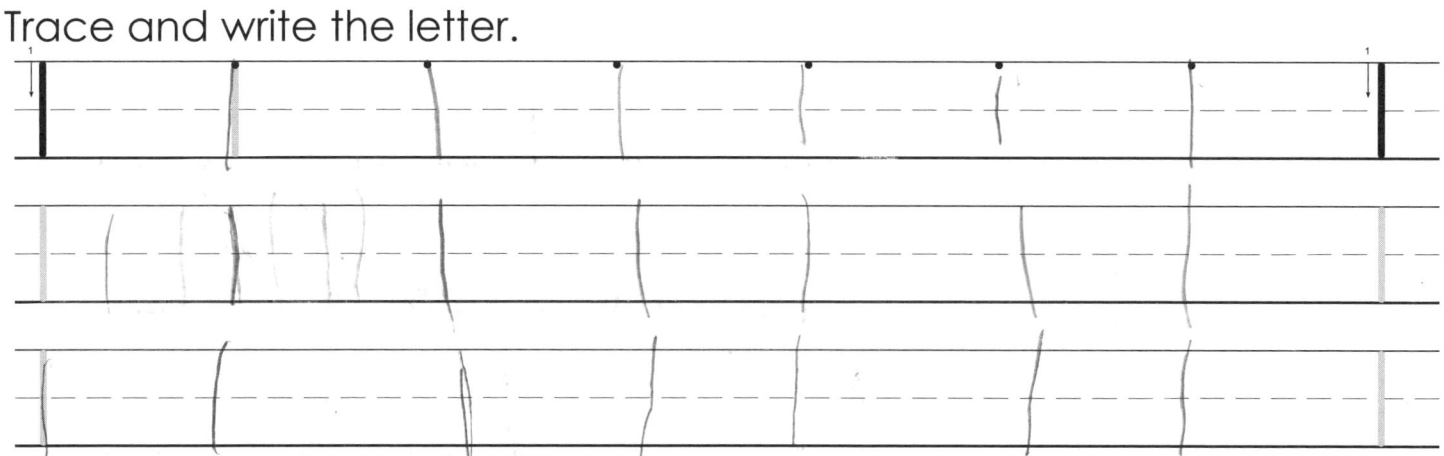

Trace and write the words.

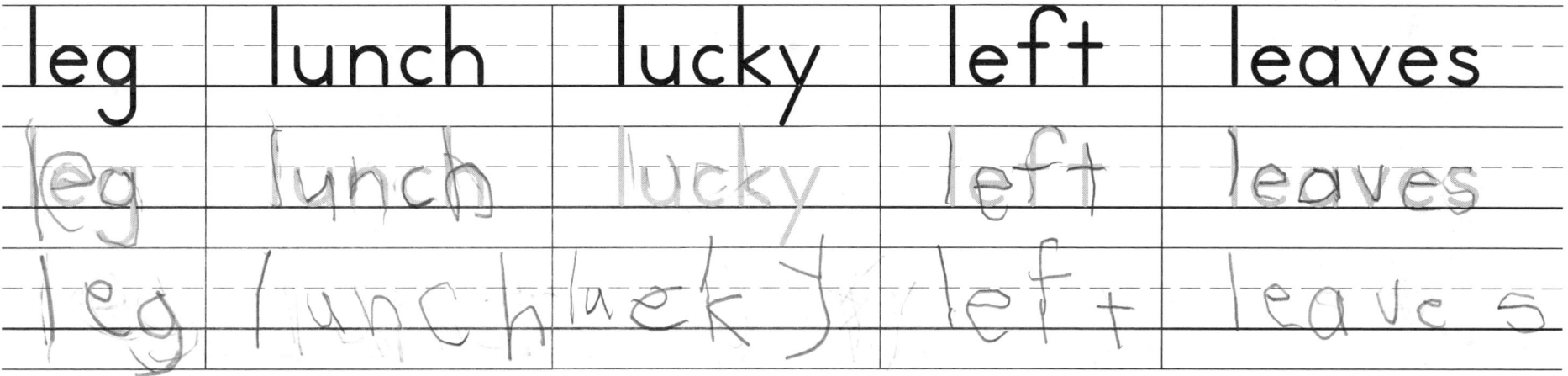

PAPER POSITION

LEFT HAND

RIGHT HAND

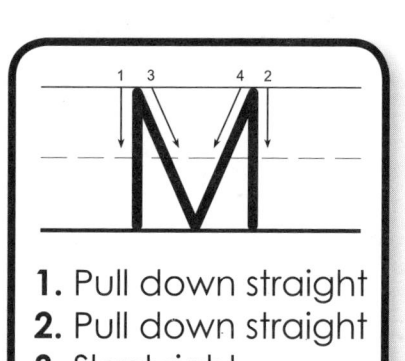

1. Pull down straight
2. Pull down straight
3. Slant right
4. Slant left

Trace and write the letter.

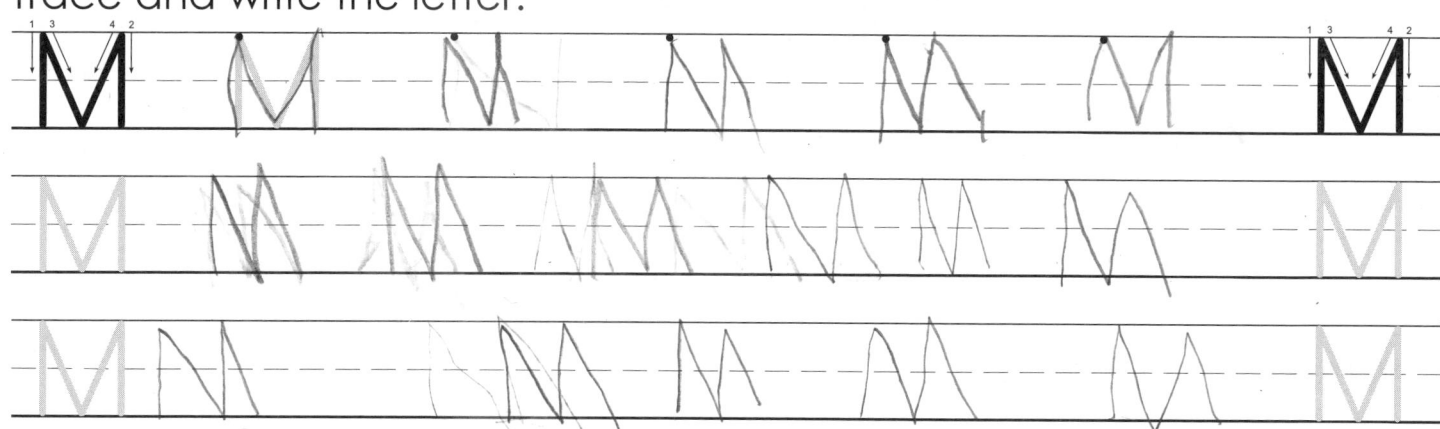

Trace and write the words. Write the sentence.

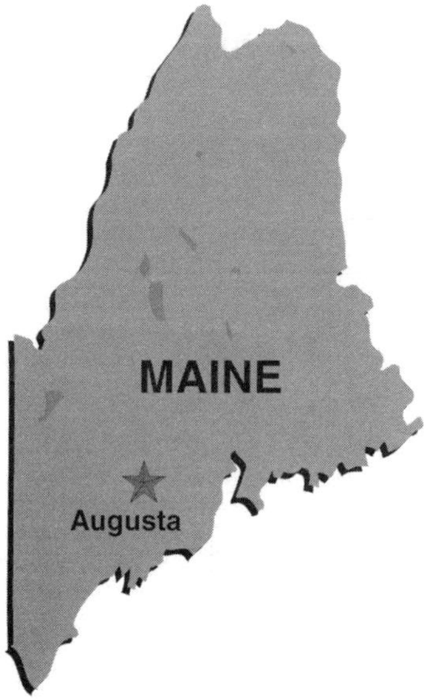

Maine	Monday	Michigan
Maine	Monday	Michigan

Memorial Day is in May.

CHECK-UP
- ☐ Letter Spacing
- ☐ Size of Letters
- ☐ Letter Forms
- ☐ Line Quality

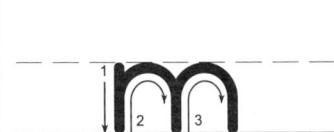

1. Pull down straight
2. Push up, curve right, pull down
3. Push up, curve right, pull down

Trace and write the letter.

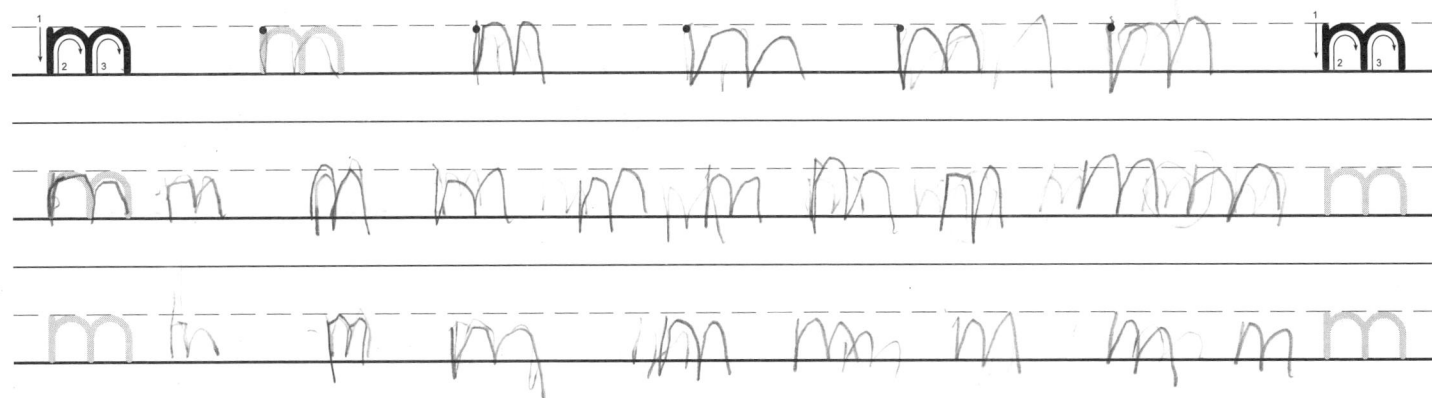

Trace and write the words. Write the sentence.

| morning | minute | money |

Mother made me mittens.

CHECK-UP
- ☐ Word Spacing
- ☐ Size of Letters
- ☐ Letter Forms
- ☐ Line Quality

Contractions

Write each contraction as two words.

isn't

she'll

he'd

won't

we'll

it's

Write the words as contractions.

he will

are not

I would

we are

can not

she is

Write the sentence.

Don't touch the stove, it's hot!

Telling Time

Look at each clock and write the time on the lines below.

_____ _____ _____ _____

What time does school start?   What time do you go to lunch?   What time do you go to bed?
_____   _____   _____

What is your favorite time of day? Why?
_____
_____
_____
_____
_____

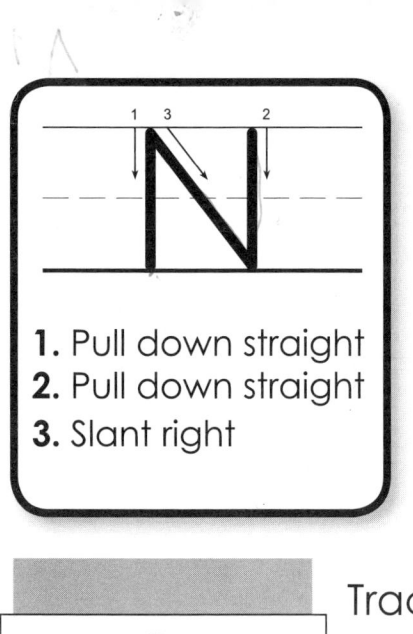

Trace and write the letter.

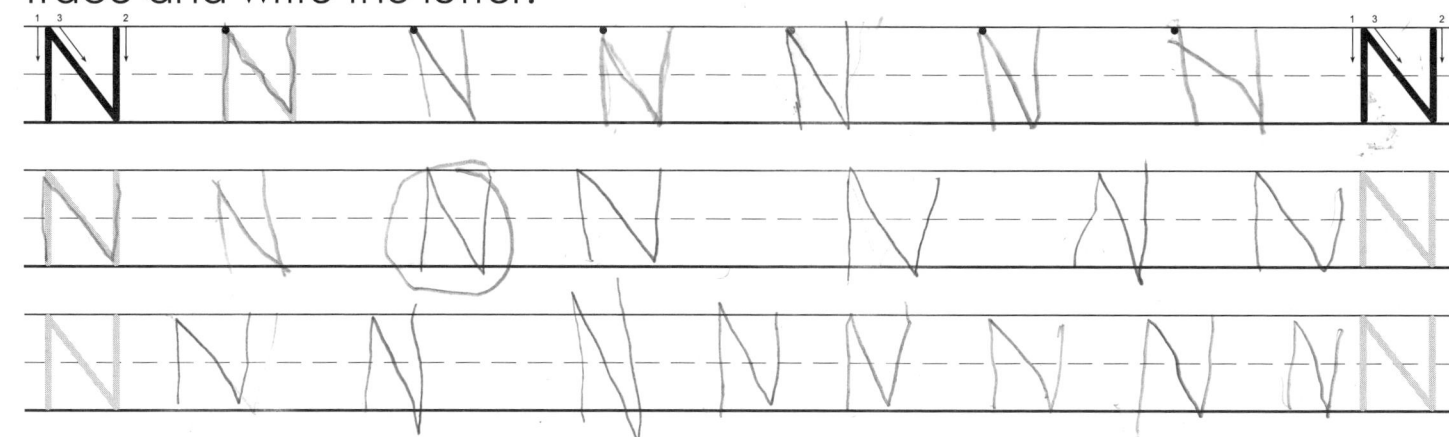

Trace and write the words. Write the sentence.

November

November	Nadia	Nicholas
November	Nadia	Nicholas
November	Nadia	Nicholas
November	Nadia	Nicholas

Nathan lives in Nevada.

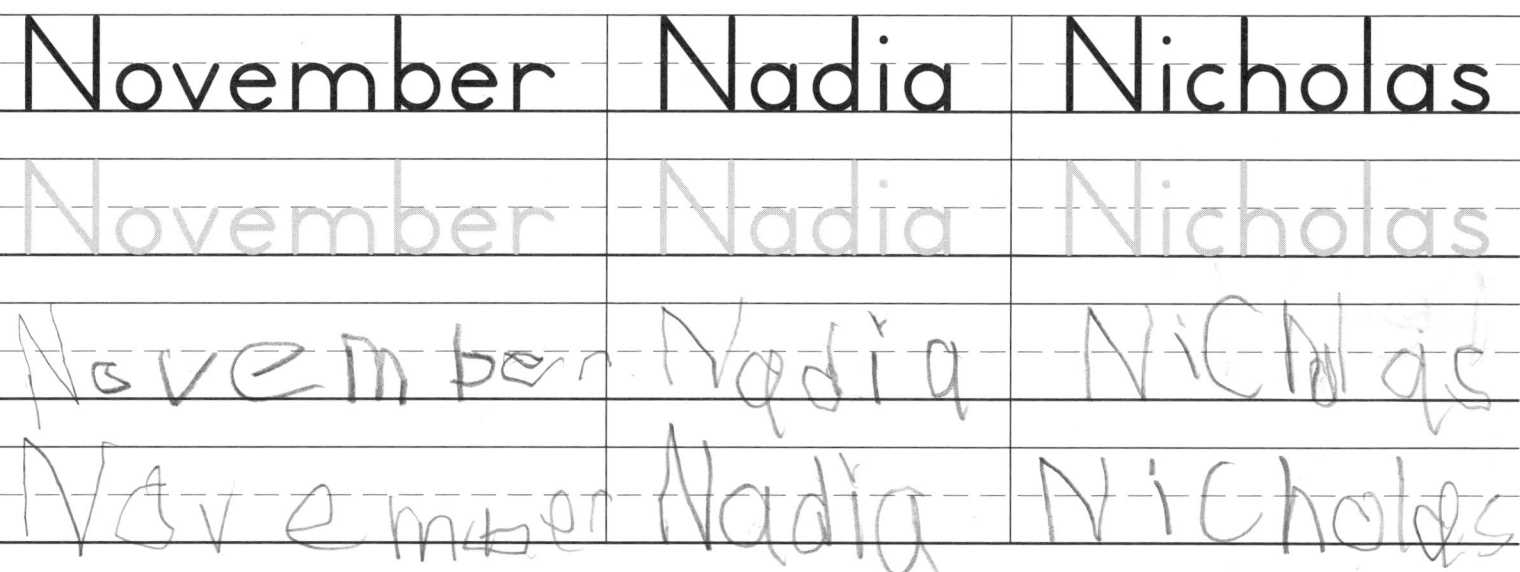

✓ **CHECK-UP**
- ☐ Letter Spacing
- ☐ Size of Letters
- ☐ Letter Forms
- ☐ Line Quality

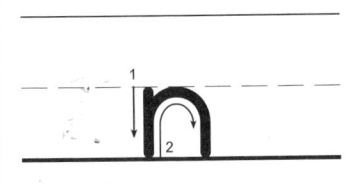

1. Pull down straight
2. Push up, curve right, pull down straight

Trace and write the letter.

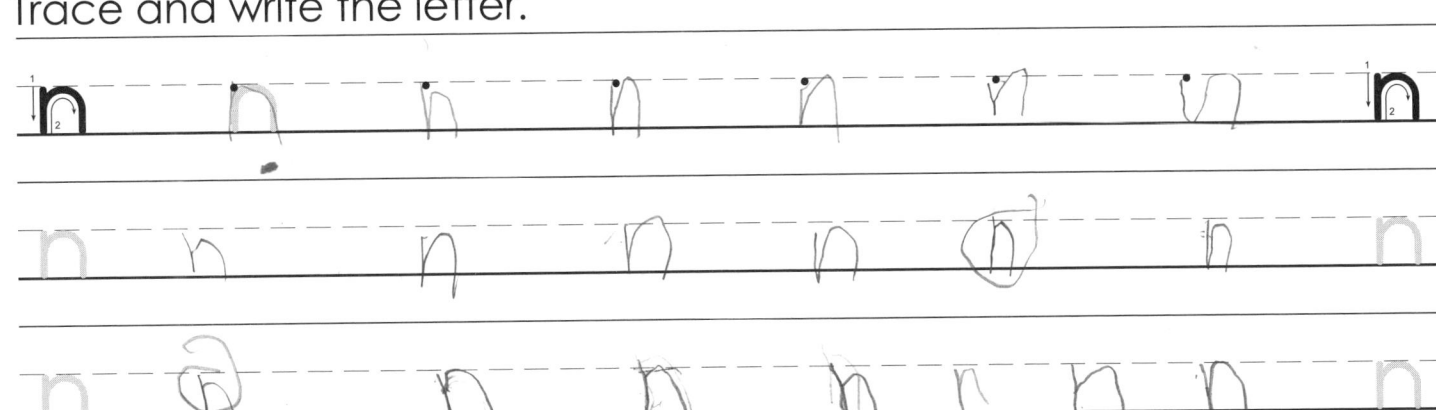

Trace and write the words. Write the sentence.

nest	night	nickel	name
nest	night	nickel	name
nest	night	nickel	name
nest	night	nickel	name

Daniel Boone was a pioneer.

Daniel Boone was a pioneer.

✓ **CHECK-UP**
☐ Word Spacing
☐ Size of Letters
☐ Letter Forms
☐ Line Quality

Writing Numbers

Write the answer to the problem. Then write the problem in words, as shown below.

Words to Know: plus   minus   equals

13 − 6 = 7

Thirteen minus six equals seven.

5 + 10 = ___

4 + 7 = ___

18 − 10 = ___

Words That Rhyme

Write one word that rhymes with each of the words below.

cat	book	pail	nap
_____	_____	_____	_____
_____	_____	_____	_____
_____	_____	_____	_____

Write the word next to each picture. Then draw a line to the words that rhyme.

moon

hat

dog

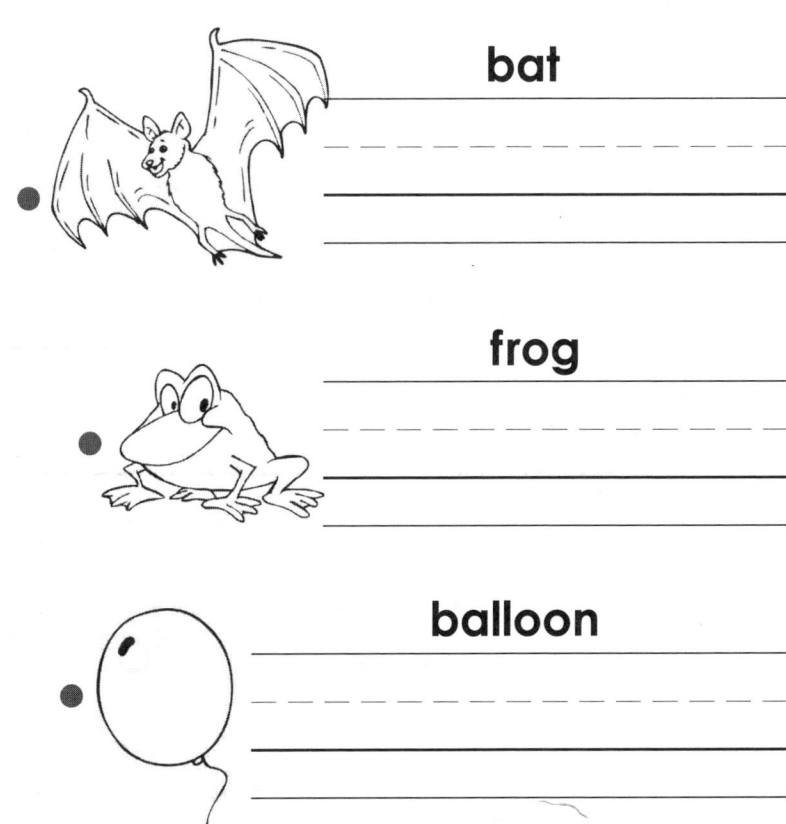

bat

frog

balloon

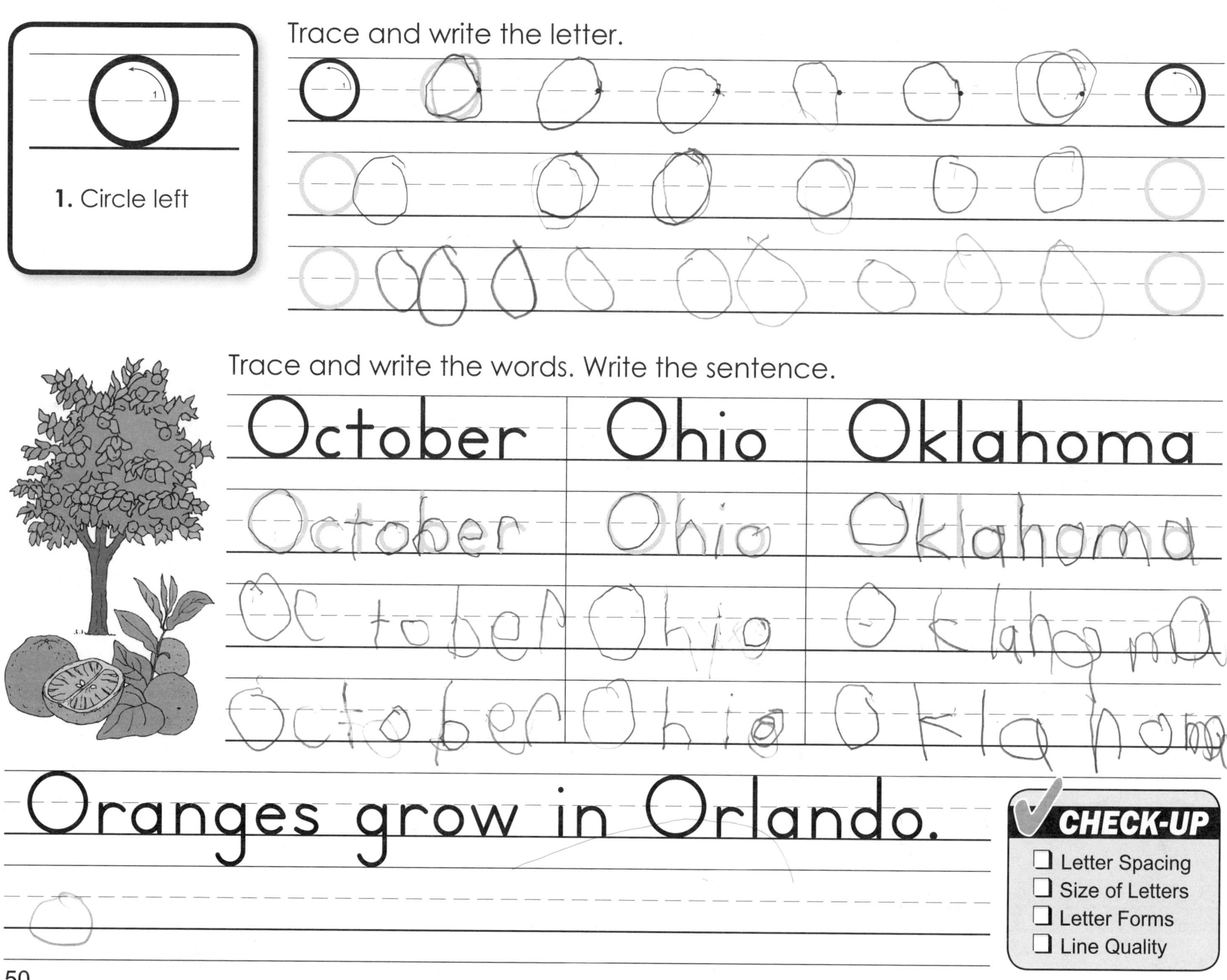

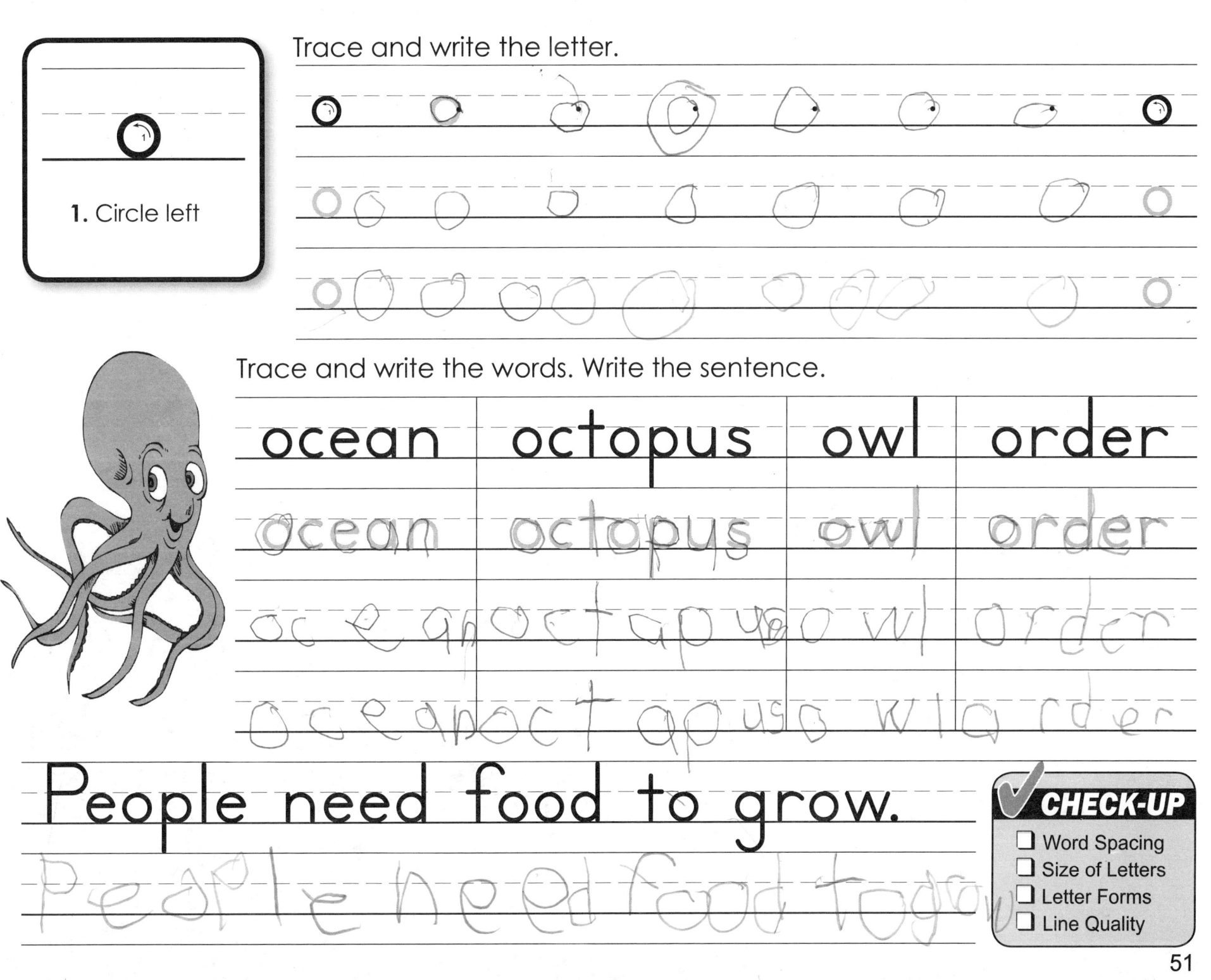

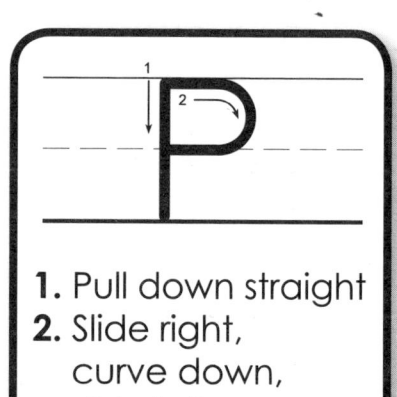

1. Pull down straight
2. Slide right, curve down, slide left

Trace and write the letter.

Trace and write the words. Write the sentence.

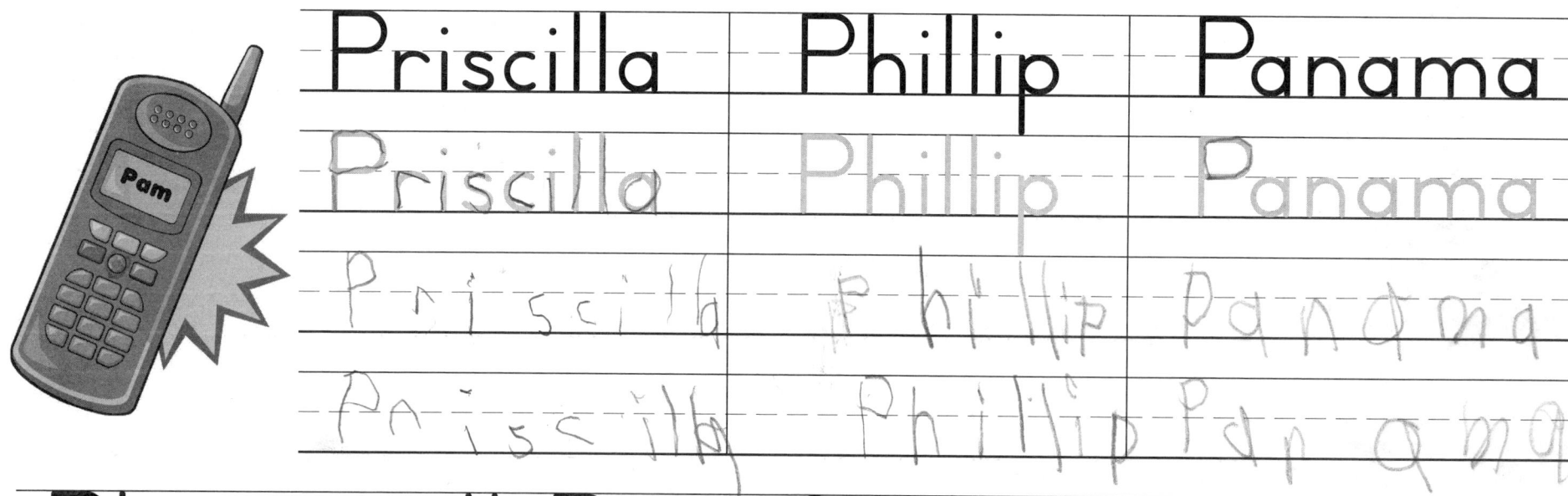

Priscilla   Phillip   Panama

Please call Pam for Paula.

✓ **CHECK-UP**
☐ Letter Spacing
☐ Size of Letters
☐ Letter Forms
☐ Line Quality

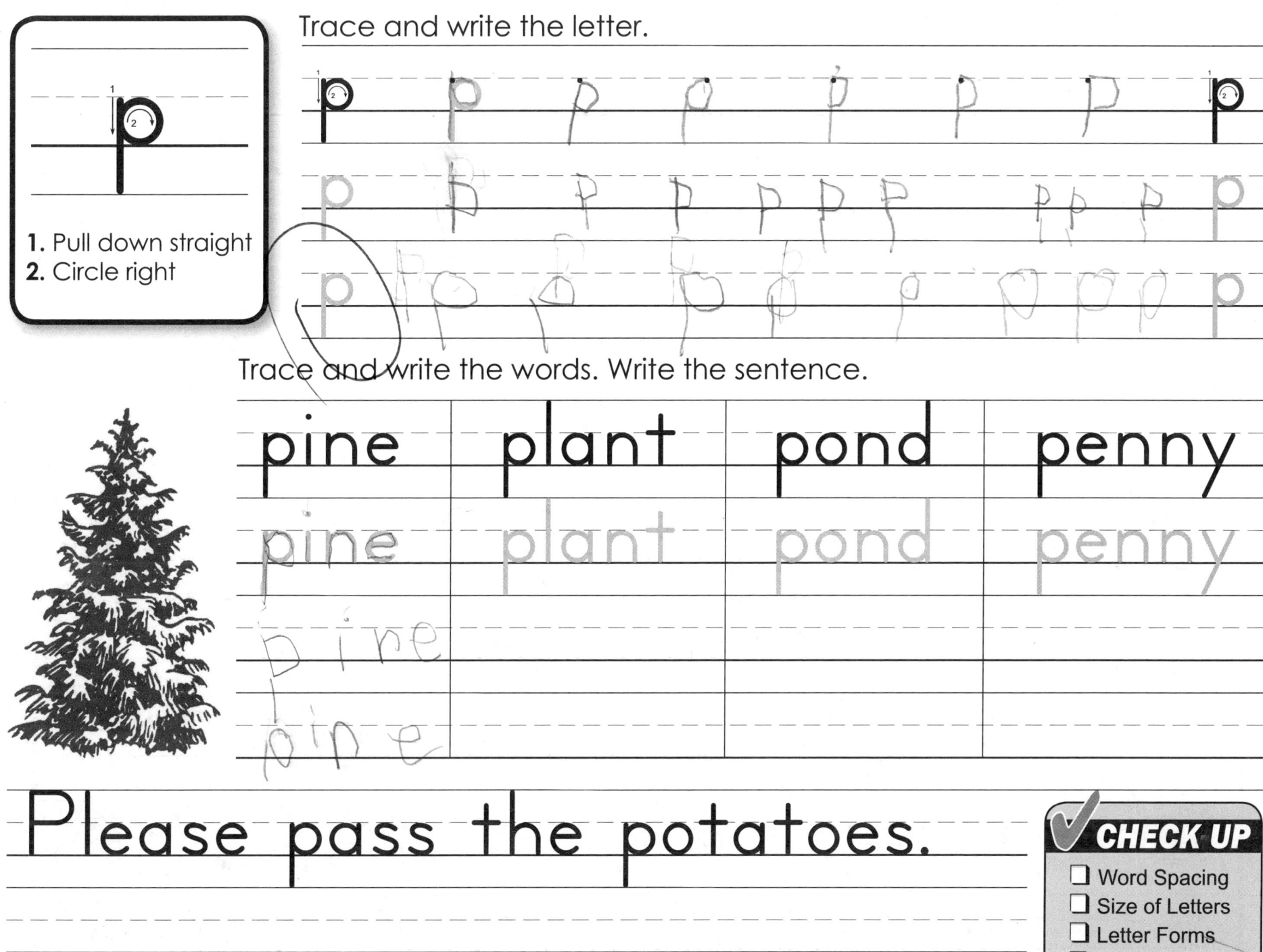

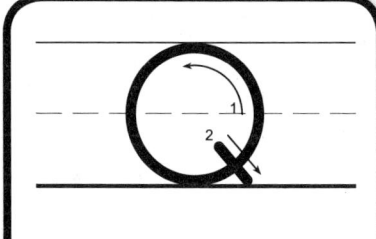

1. Circle left
2. Slant right

Trace and write the letter.

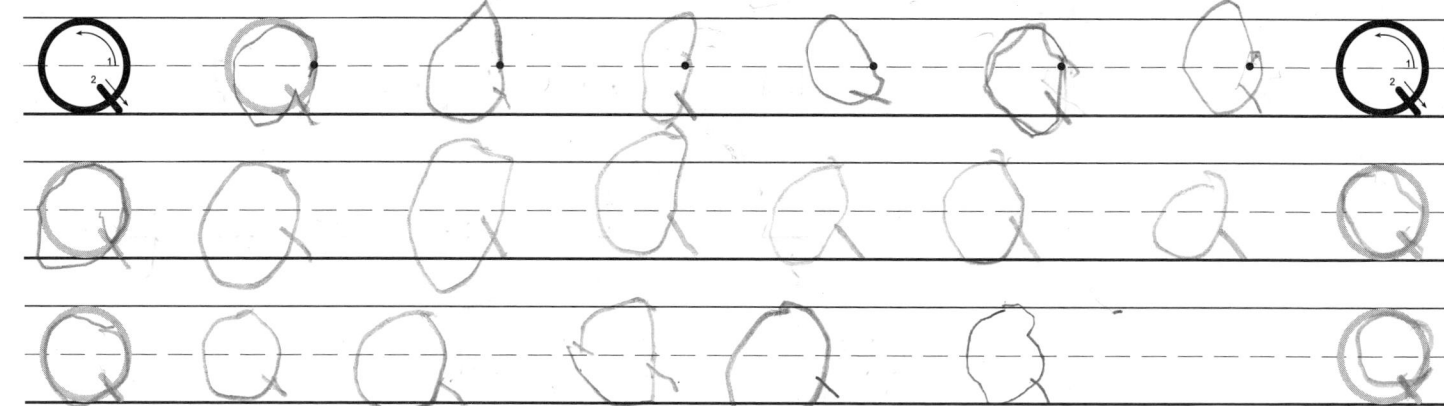

Write the words.

Quinton   Quincy

Quebec   Quinn

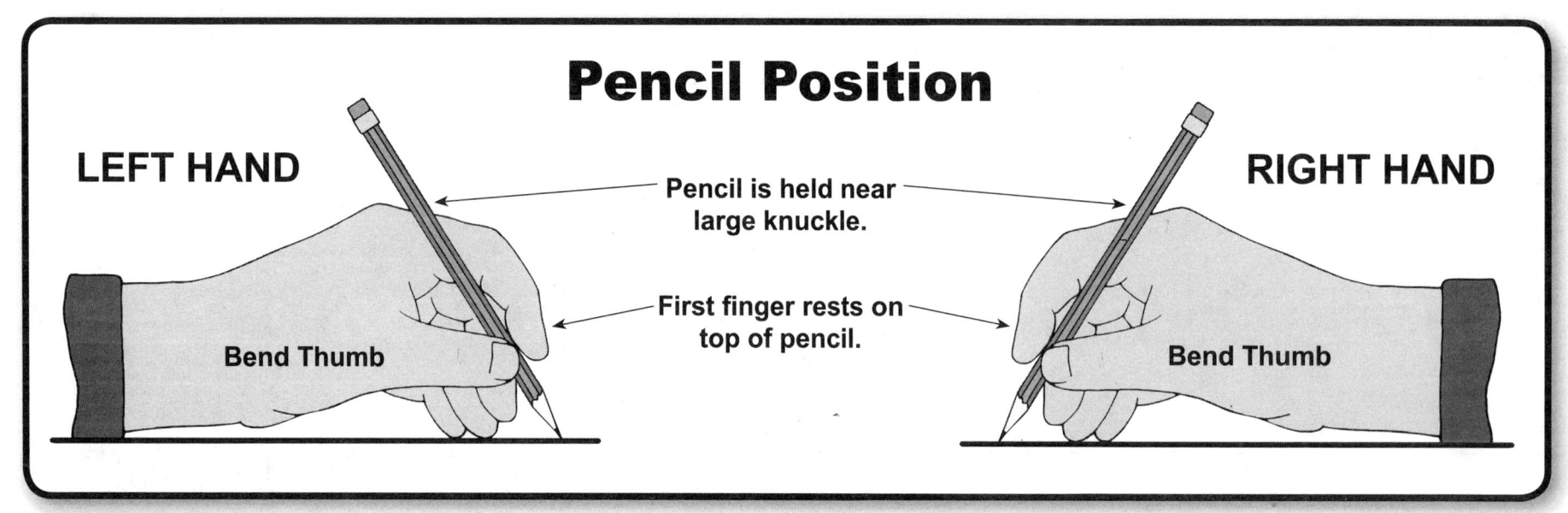

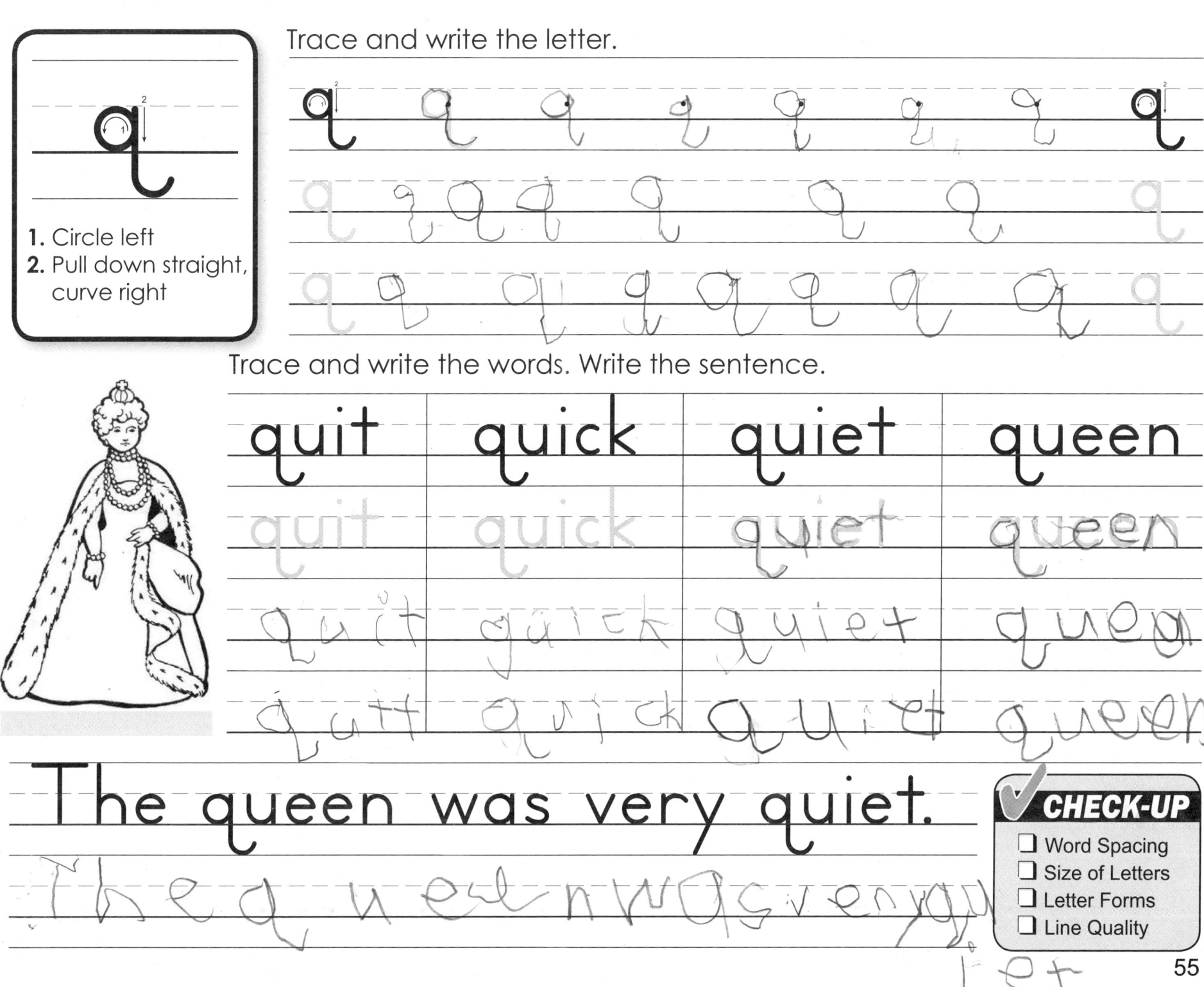

Days of the Week

Write the days of the week in order.

Thursday   Sunday   Wednesday   Tuesday   Saturday   Monday   Friday

1. _____

2. _____

3. _____

4. _____

5. _____

6. _____

7. _____

Unscramble the day: **uadSrtay**

_____

What is your favorite day of the week? Why?

_____
_____
_____
_____

56

Compound Words

Trace the words. Then combine each word with a word from the box to create a compound word. Write the new word.

Original Word	New Word (Compound Word)
cow	
rain	
after	
lady	
butter	
foot	
birth	
your	

bug

day

fly

bow

ball

noon

boy

self

57

1. Pull down straight
2. Slide right, curve down, slide left
3. Slant right

Trace and write the letter.

R R R R

R R

R R

Trace and write the words. Write the sentence.

Rome	Rebecca	Richard
Rome	Rebecca	Richard

Is Ron from Rhode Island?

CHECK-UP
☐ Letter Spacing
☐ Size of Letters
☐ Letter Forms
☐ Line Quality

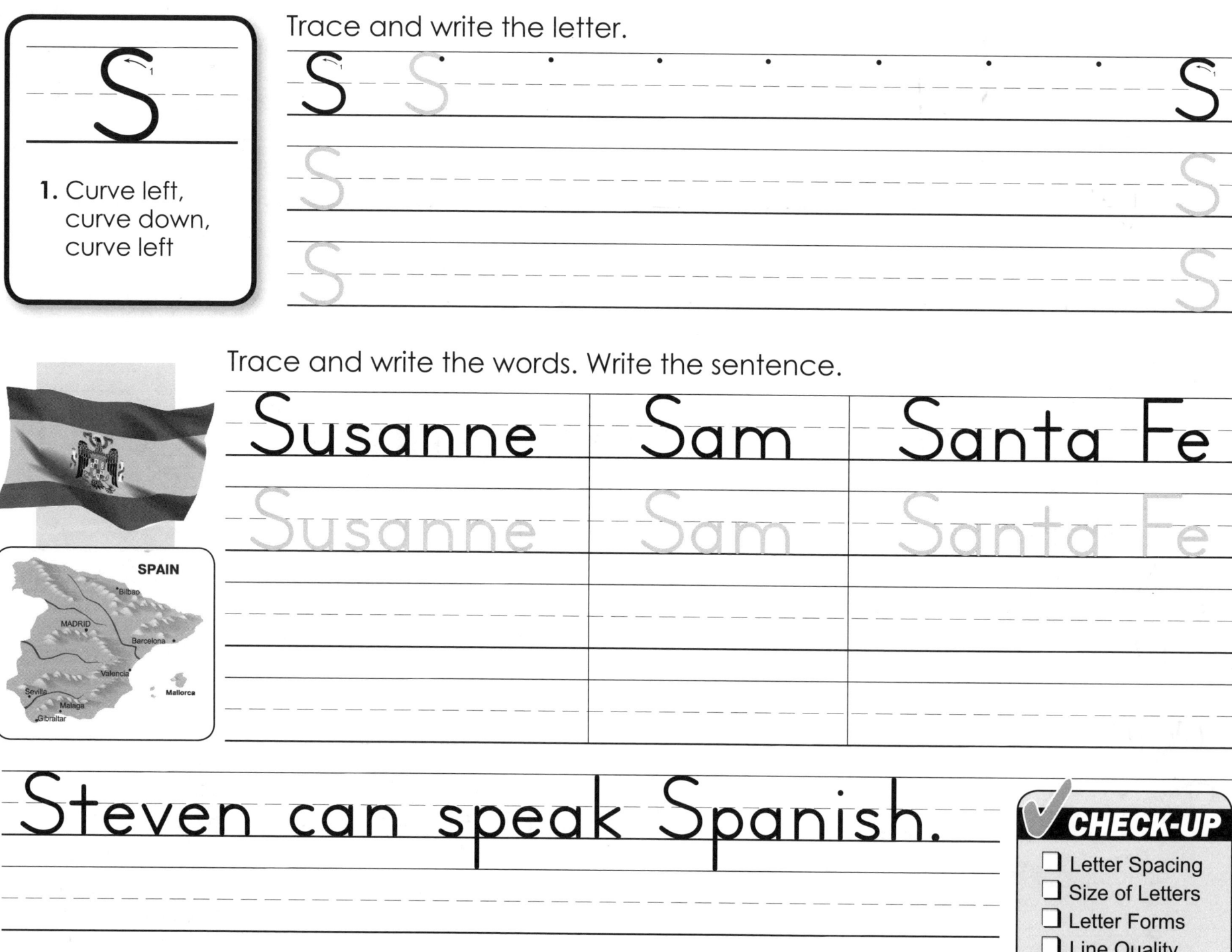

s

1. Curve left, curve down, curve left

Trace and write the letter.

s s s

Trace and write the words. Write the sentence.

seals	sister	shoes	seven
seals	sister	shoes	seven

Susan saw seven silly seals.

✓ CHECK-UP
- ☐ Word Spacing
- ☐ Size of Letters
- ☐ Letter Forms
- ☐ Line Quality

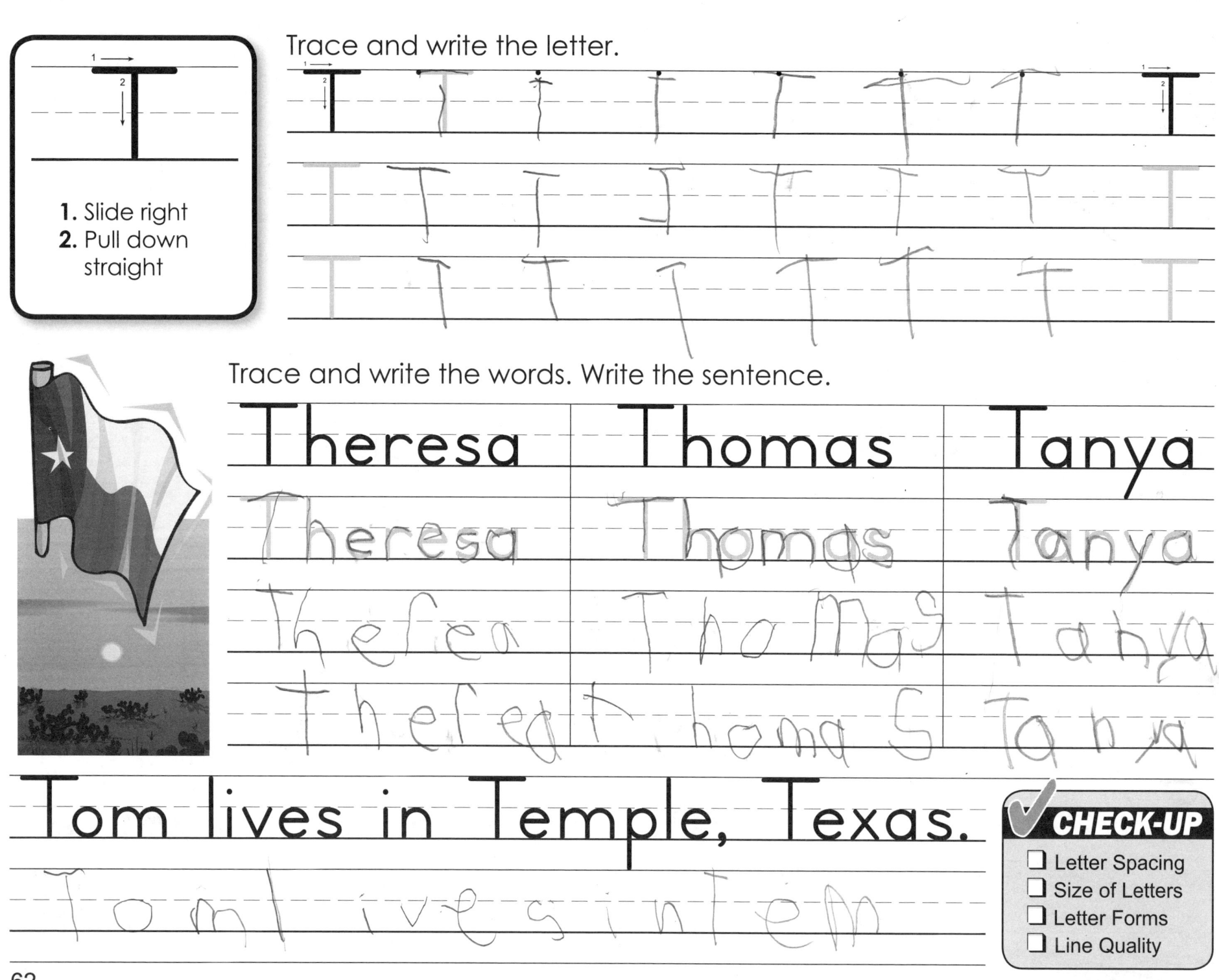

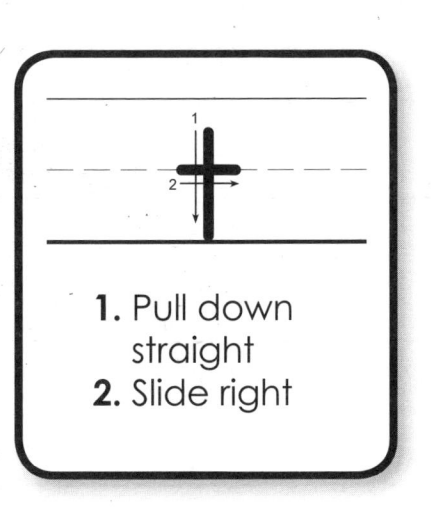

1. Pull down straight
2. Slide right

Trace and write the letter.

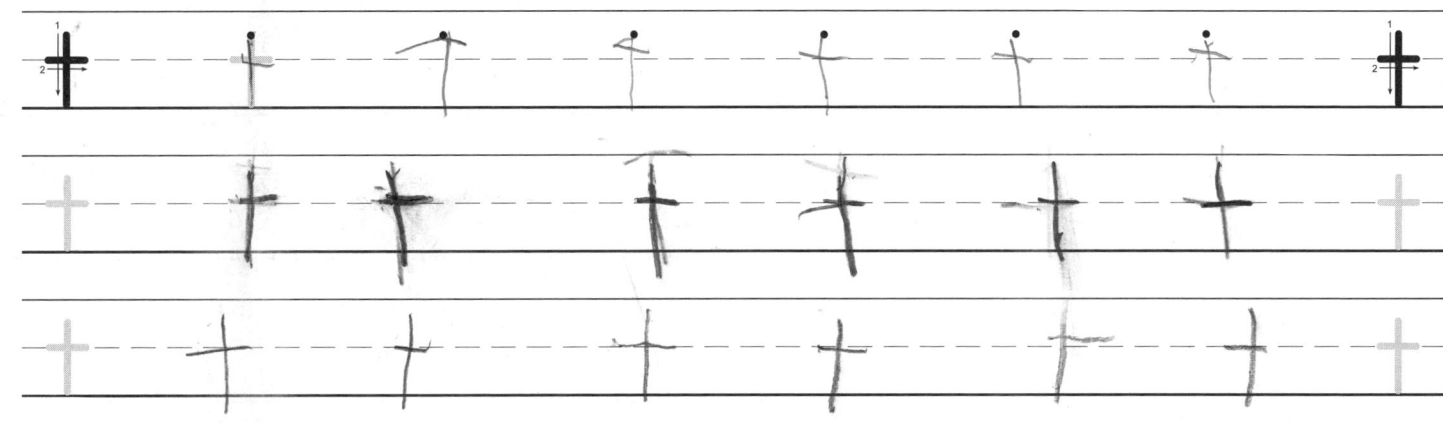

Trace and write the words. Write the sentence.

tree	truth	thanks	time
tree	truth	thanks	time
tree	truth	thanks	time
tree	truth	thanks	time

Tate and Rita are twins.

Tate and Rita are twins

CHECK-UP
☐ Word Spacing
☐ Size of Letters
☐ Letter Forms
☐ Line Quality

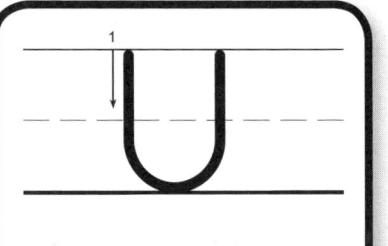

Trace and write the letter.

1. Pull down straight, curve right, push up

Write the sentence.

The letters U.S.A. stand for

United States of America.

CHECK-UP
- ☐ Letter Spacing
- ☐ Size of Letters
- ☐ Letter Forms
- ☐ Line Quality

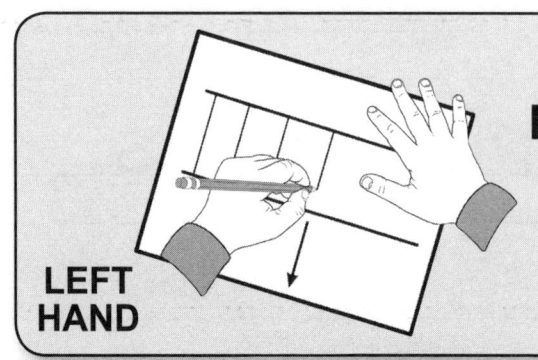

PAPER POSITION

LEFT HAND

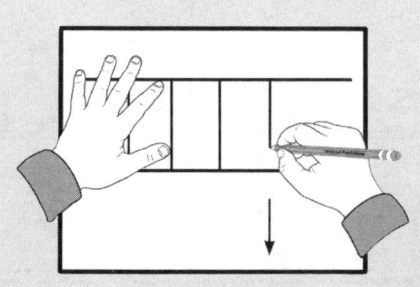

RIGHT HAND

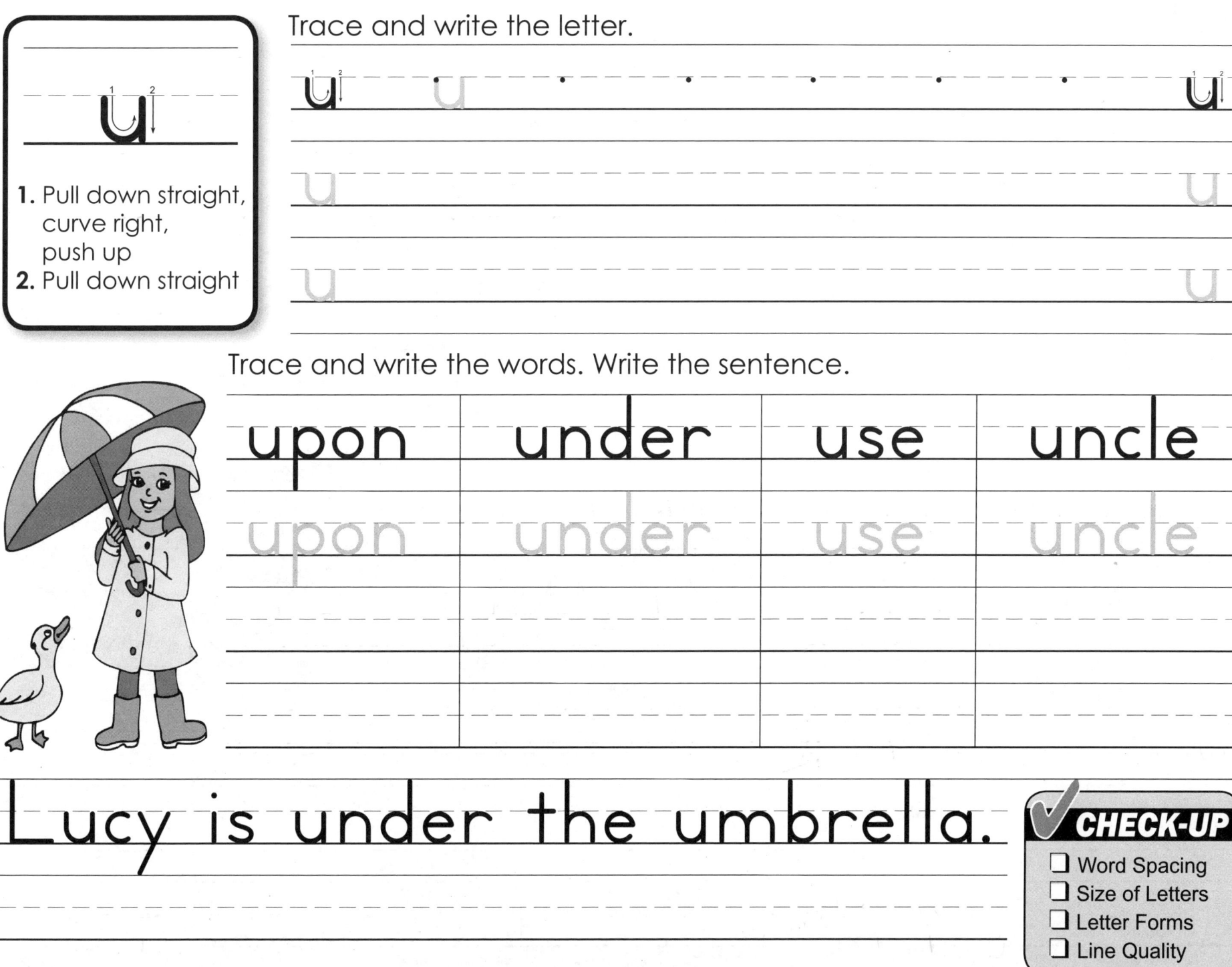

Number Practice

Write the numbers in order from smallest to largest.

83   17   56   29   43   70

Write the answers to the following questions.

How many people are in your class?

How many letters are in the alphabet?

In what year were you born?

How many states are in the United States?

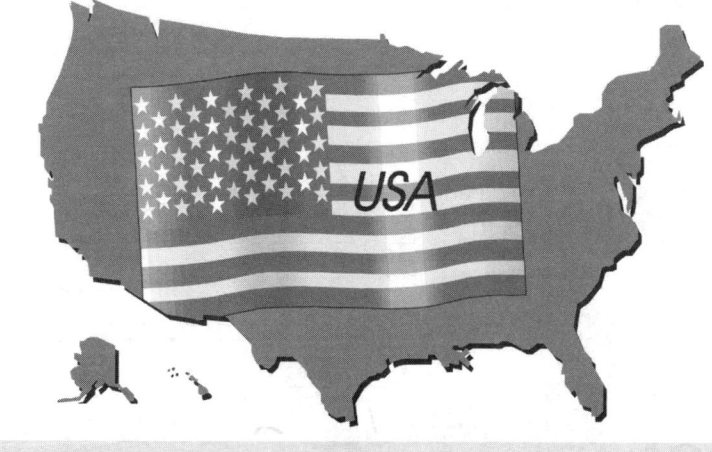

What is your favorite number? Why?

Writing Numbers

Write the answer to the problem. Then write the problem in words, as shown below.

Words to Know

plus   minus   equals

12 + 3 = 15

Twelve plus three equals fifteen.

8 − 6 = ___

10 + 4 = ___

16 − 9 = ___

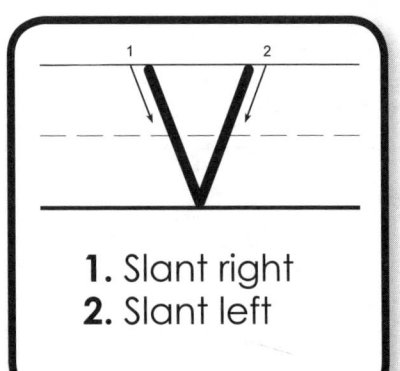

1. Slant right
2. Slant left

Trace and write the letter.

Trace and write the words. Write the sentence.

Valerie	Vincent	Virginia	Victor
Valerie	Vincent	Virginia	Victor
Valerie	Vincent	Virginia	Vicor
Valere	Vicent	Vieinia	Vicor

Veronica lives in Vermont.

Veronica lives in Vermot

✓ CHECK-UP
☐ Letter Spacing
☐ Size of Letters
☐ Letter Forms
☐ Line Quality

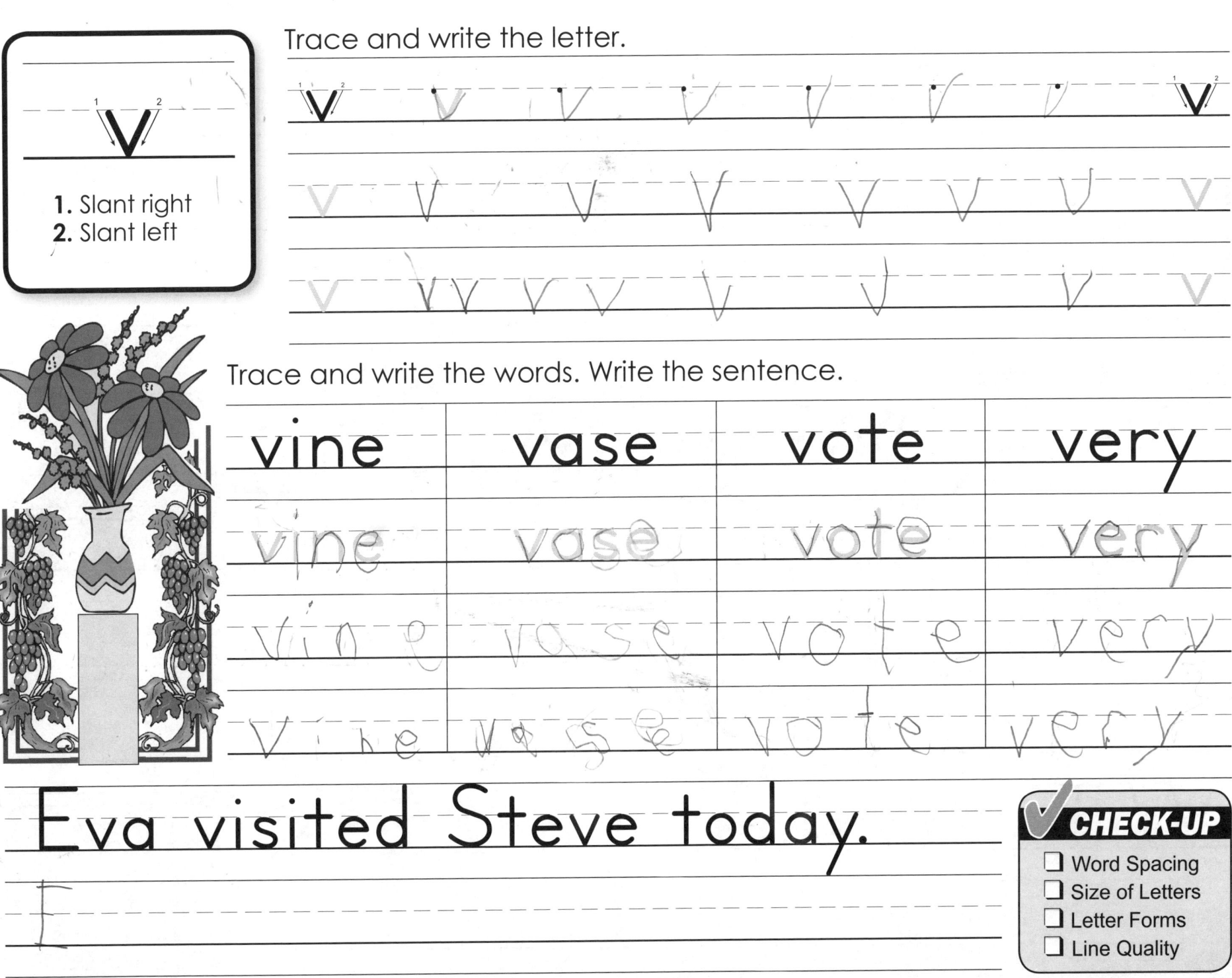

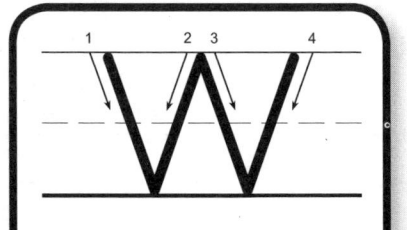

1. Slant right
2. Slant left
3. Slant right
4. Slant left

Trace and write the letter.

Trace and write the words. Write the sentence.

| Walter | Wendy | Wyoming | Will |

Will Wes sing with Wade?

CHECK-UP
☐ Letter Spacing
☐ Size of Letters
☐ Letter Forms
☐ Line Quality

Trace and write the letter.

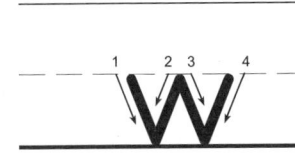

1. Slant right
2. Slant left
3. Slant right
4. Slant left

Trace and write the words. Write the sentence.

water	who	white	would
water	who	white	would
water	who	white	would
water	who	white	would

Wow! Wayne won a watch.

CHECK-UP
- ☐ Word Spacing
- ☐ Size of Letters
- ☐ Letter Forms
- ☐ Line Quality

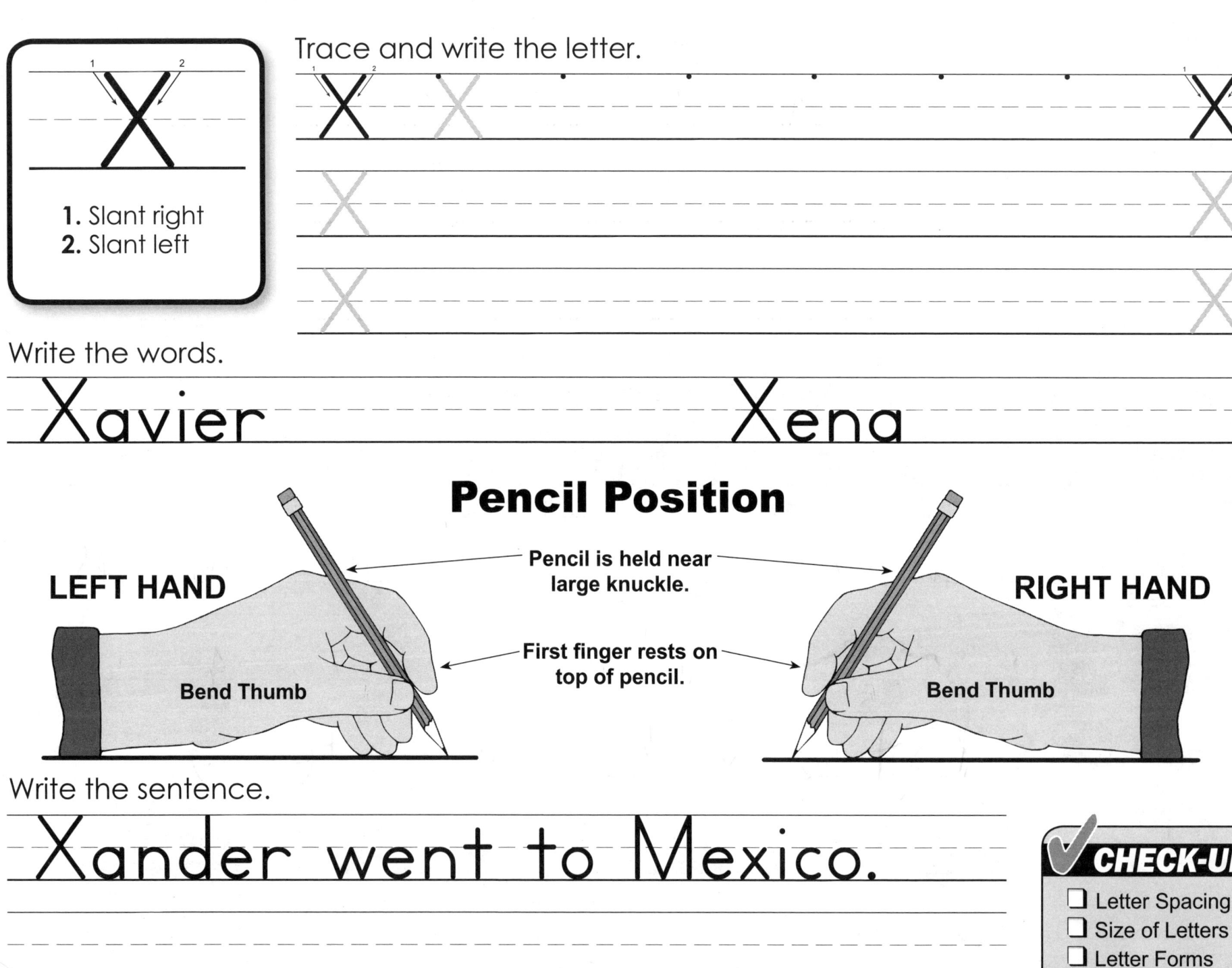

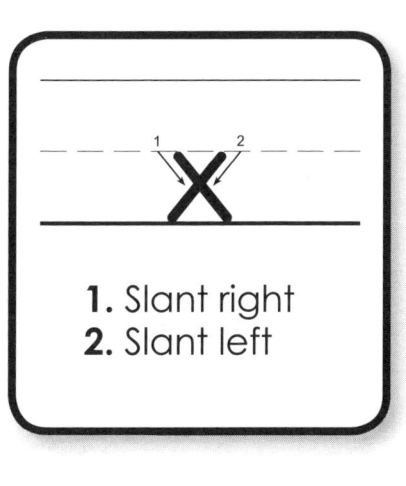

1. Slant right
2. Slant left

Trace and write the letter.

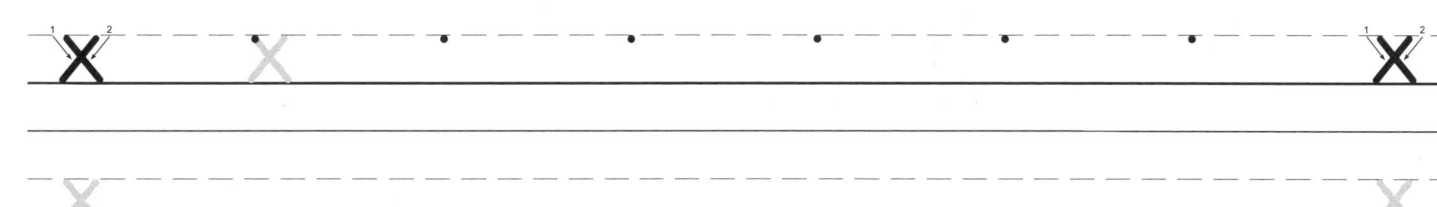

Write the words.

Texas   exit   fox

Find the correct path.

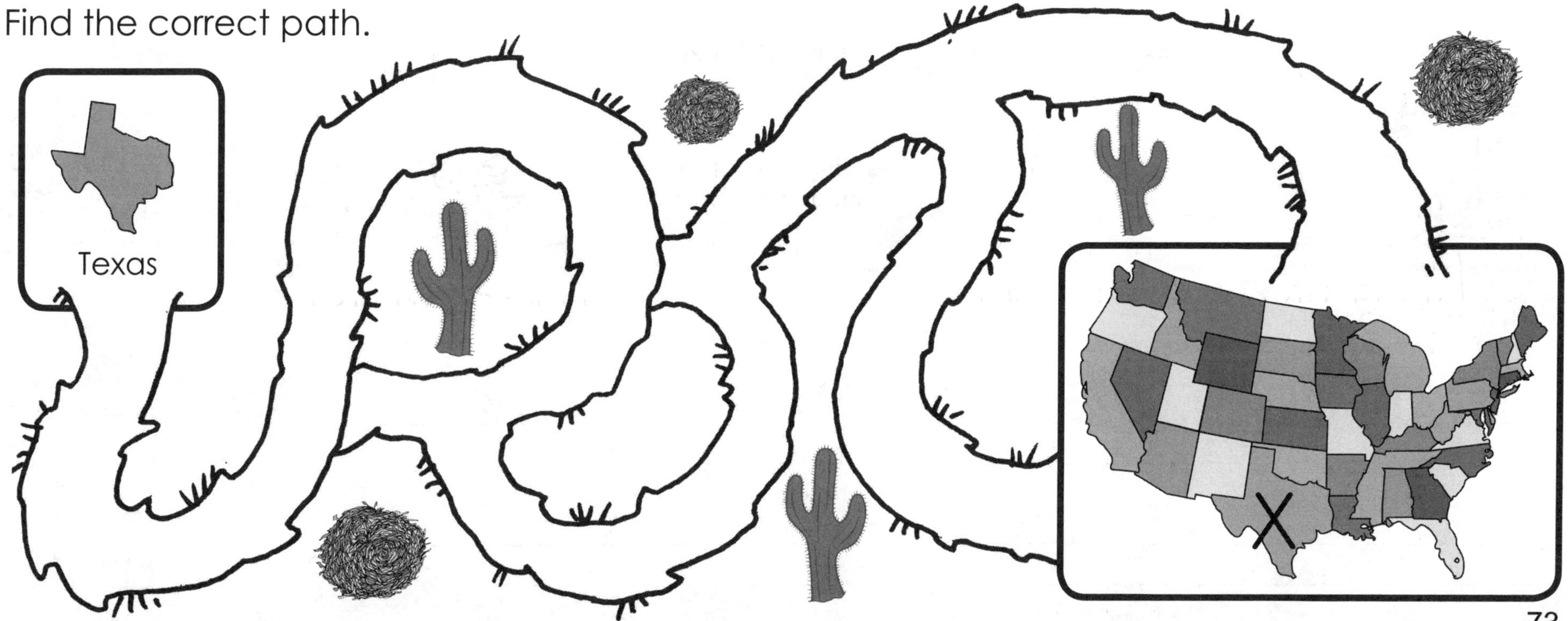

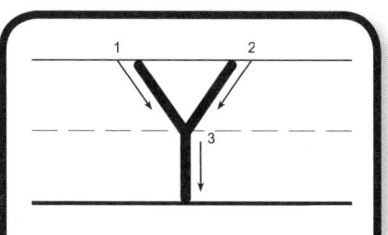

1. Slant right
2. Slant left
3. Pull down straight

Trace and write the letter.

Write the words.

Yvette   Yolanda

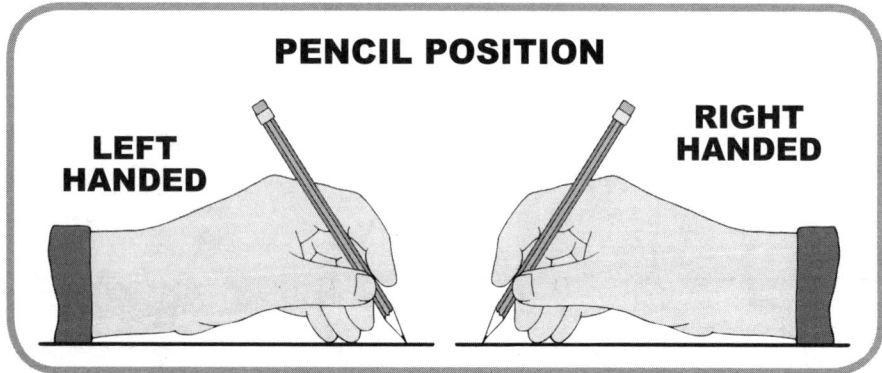

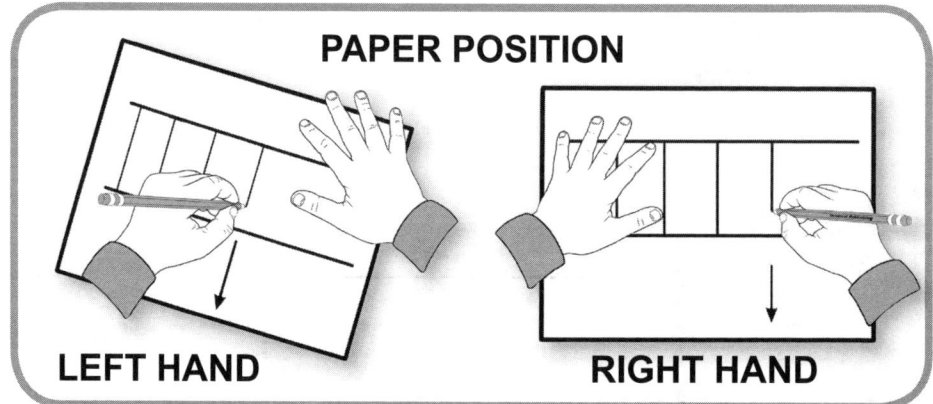

Write the sentence.

You can go to New York.

CHECK-UP
☐ Letter Spacing
☐ Size of Letters
☐ Letter Forms
☐ Line Quality

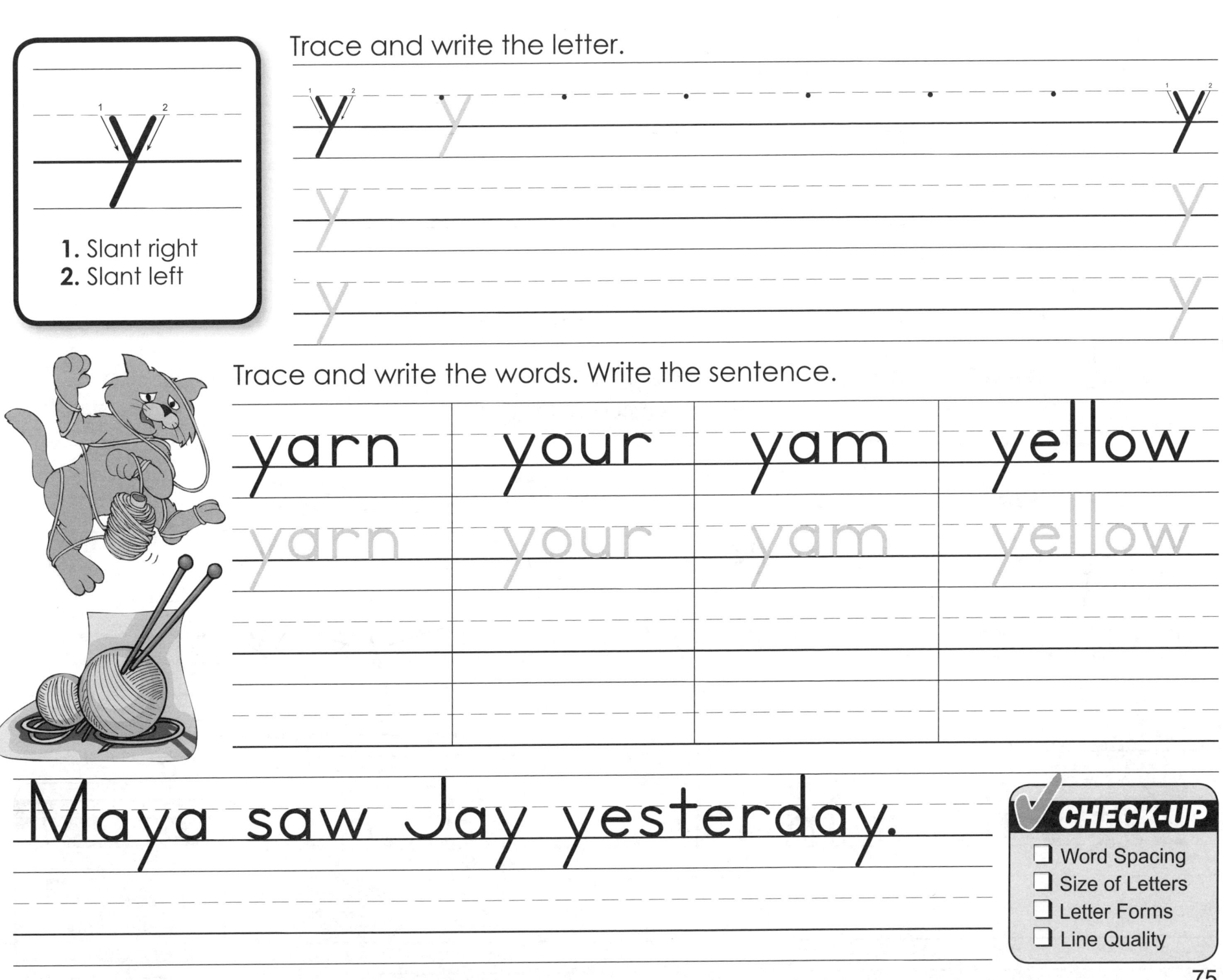

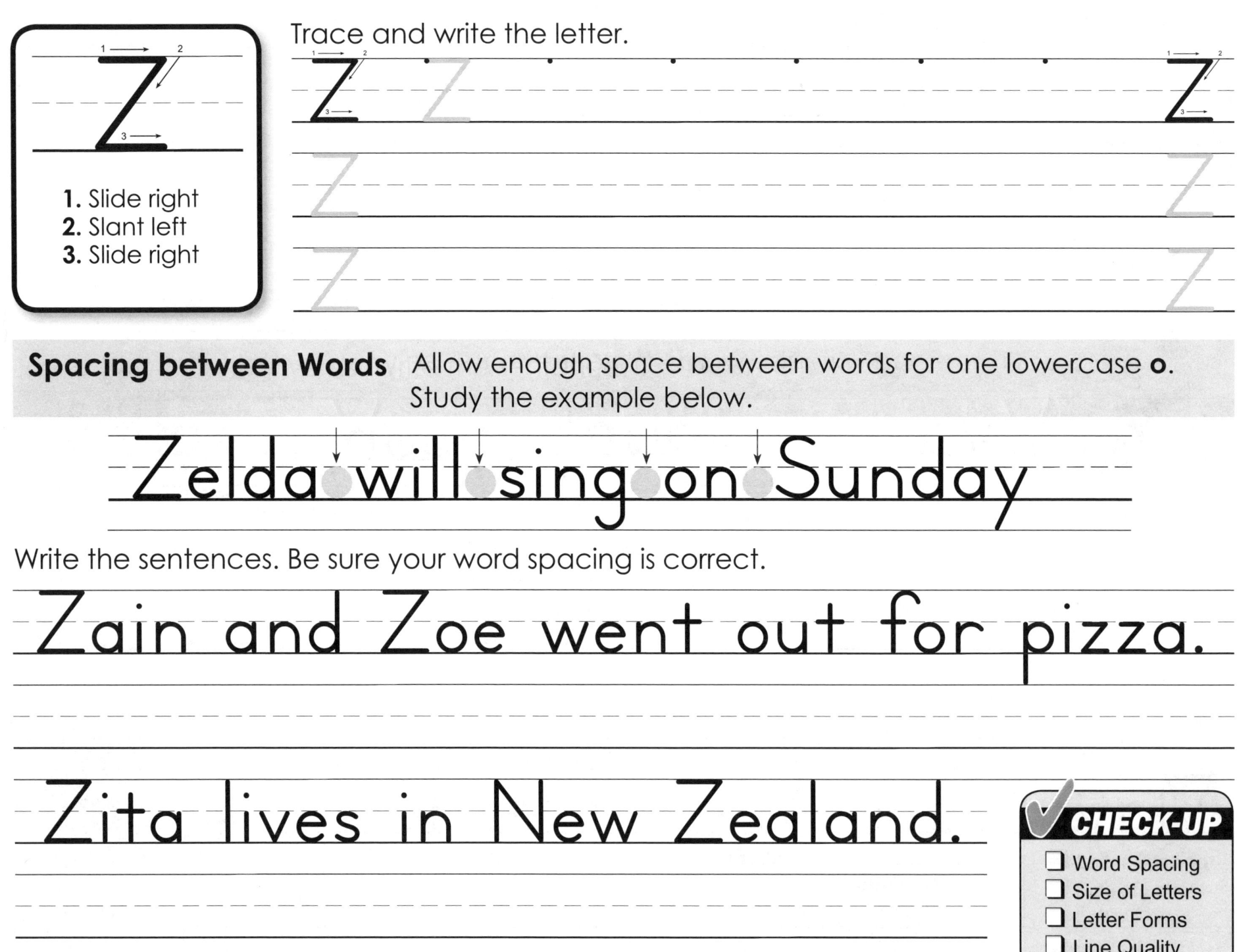

Z

1. Slide right
2. Slant left
3. Slide right

Trace and write the letter.

Trace and write the words. Write the sentence.

zero	zipper	zoom	zigzag
zero	zipper	zoom	zigzag

ZEBRA

Zoe saw zebras at the zoo.

CHECK-UP
☐ Word Spacing
☐ Size of Letters
☐ Letter Forms
☐ Line Quality

77

My Picture and Story

Draw a picture. On the next page, write a story about your picture.

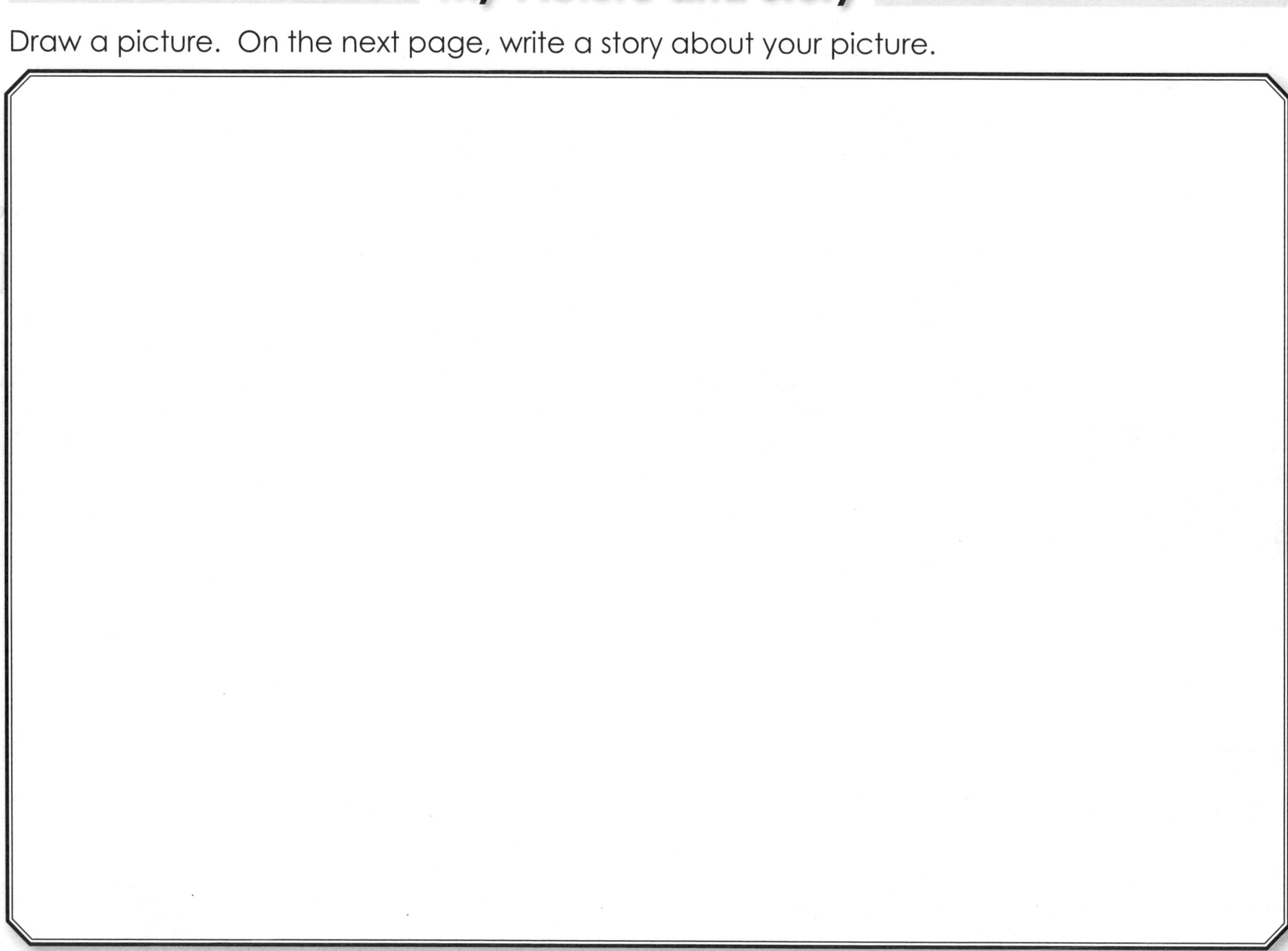

Post Test

Stop, look, and listen
before you cross the street.
Use your eyes and use your ears
before you use your feet.

Write the sentences.

✓ CHECK-UP
- ☐ Letter Spacing
- ☐ Size of Letters
- ☐ Letter Forms
- ☐ Line Quality